T0391056

Just Passing Through

(as we all are)

Date published: September 2024

Written, edited, cover design and published by: George C. Squires (gsquires1959@gmail.com)

Memories also recalled and created by: Good friends and family

"The two most important days of your life are the day you are born

and the day you find out why."

-Mark Twain

Introduction

A couple of years ago, my dad suggested that I write a memoir for future generations, something for the kids and grandkids to remember me by. Every individual possesses a unique set of narratives, circumstances, peaks and valleys that shape them. These are my stories; some evoke happiness, while others bring pain and I would really prefer not to revisit them. However, they're important to understand who I am and how these situations shaped me. I've strived to be truthful and accurate; using real places, real events and real names, but only first names. Also, I'm weaving in some humor and *life lessons* that I've picked up along my journey.

As you travel through life various individuals, locations and experiences serve as catalysts driving you forward, akin to the way the wind propels a sail. Nevertheless, individuals possess the rudder of free will and personal choice, which also guides them towards positive or negative outcomes. There were times when I hit the rocks and ran aground, along with periods of smooth, happy sailing. *The reality is that you control very little in life besides yourself; it's about managing what's thrown at you.* This is my story.

George Calvin Squires

Oh Boy, I'm in Big Trouble…!

Chapter 1

The 60's - Normal…For the Most Part

Chapter 2

The 70's - Big Trouble and Then Some

Chapter 3

The 80's - Road to Enlightenment

Chapter 4

The 90's - Growing a Career & Family

Chapter 5

The 2000's - Regrouping & New Opportunities

Getting Back to Life

Doing Business

Herding Cats, I mean Kids

Fun Times for Us

Business…the Good, the Bad and the Ugly

Going, Going, Gone

Starting my Start-up

The Crash of 2009

Chapter 6

The 2010's - Growing, Selling, Retiring, Love & Adventure

Dating and Relationships

Growing PWT

Beach Life and Meeting New Friends

Laguna Beach, Surfs Up

Flying Kites and Traveling

The Kids Finding Their Paths

Big Changes in 17 so Don't Blink

No More Alarm Clocks

The Bucket List and the Big Ask

Chapter 7

The 2020's - Covid, Mom, Dad, Wedding and Adventures

Covid is Here but Life Doesn't Stop

Recovering, Wedding Planning and Travel

Big World Here We Come

Bike and Boat Trips, then Getting Hitched

Home, Back to Normal with Good Friends

My Dad

Life's Safety Nets

Remembering the Past but Looking Forward

Today

Oh Boy, I'm in Big Trouble...!

THE SUN HAD JUST GONE DOWN, I could see my breath and feel the cold in my bones on that late February night before we arrived at the Kirkwood apartment. My new friends, whom I had just met an hour earlier, said the product looked good and pulled out a stack of cash to hand to me...but then I said, "I'm not doing business with you, Curt is." Curt was the guy who had initially orchestrated this deal. Just as the money touched his hands, the front and back doors burst open with a loud bang. Glass and wood flew as a half a dozen St. Louis county police officers charged in, guns drawn and wearing bulletproof vests. I immediately raised my hands and informed them that I had a gun tucked in my pants, loaded, and the safety was off.

I was taken to the police station and placed in an interrogation room for several hours. One of the officers entered the room holding my wallet. He proceeded to throw my driver's license, money and remaining contents into the trash can, one by one, removing each item separately, I believe for dramatic effect. Then he said, "You won't need a wallet or driver's license for the next ten years." That was of course, the "bad" cop. But then the "good" cop came in and said that he knew I was a good kid, and would do the right thing. Which was to name and set up my connection, the "Big Fish" that I was getting my stuff from.

My supplier was Jerome, he had long hair, wore cowboy boots and always drove a new Corvette. If you crossed him, he would kill you with a heroin overdose and have his associates dispose of your body in a remote country ditch. So, in my opinion turning on him wasn't a good option. By the way, Jerome retired, moved to Florida and bought a hotel in Fort Lauderdale. In 2013, at the age of fifty-nine he passed away from cancer.

After spending most of the night with the bad cop/good cop messing with me they finally put me in a holding cell. It wasn't the first time in my life. That morning, I was released and charges would come later. They followed me around the clock anticipating that I would lead them to other people. Well, I was just a seventeen-year-old kid but my understanding of the legal system, even at that early age, surpassed that of most individuals. This wasn't my first time in trouble and I was aware that saying anything to these cops wouldn't help me. "*Anything you say can and will be used against you,*" how clear can that be! I once saw a fish mounted on a wall with a plaque underneath that said "if I had kept my mouth shut, I wouldn't be here." You may want to take note of that as a life lesson since it can apply to many situations that you find yourself in.

I was certain that the news had spread throughout the criminal community of my arrest, so I needed to ensure Jerome didn't think I ratted him out. The following day I went to a payphone, I suspected my home phone was tapped and there were no cell phones in 1978. I called him and shared that I didn't say anything, but I did want as much help as possible. Furthermore, I better not see any shady individuals lingering around my apartment that wanted to take me for a one-way ride in the country. The cops kept telling me that I was looking at ten years in prison, based on the array of charges against me. I told Jerome that if I received ten years, it wasn't worth keeping my mouth shut or even living. At that point he said to never contact him again, but he would have somebody contact me. The next day Ben called me and I met someone who would help me survive this storm.

But I'm jumping ahead; here's my whole story.

Chapter 1

The 60's - Normal…For the Most Part

I WAS BORN IN PHOENIX, ARIZONA, on November 4, 1959, to Carl and Irene. In 1959, McDonald's opened its 100th location. Later in life, I would taste test Big Macs in eleven countries across four continents (so far), by the way they all taste the same. That year a first-class stamp cost four cents, the average annual income in the U.S. was $5,016 and two additional stars were added to the American flag.

Genesis

Nobody is born without some history and lineage. Some people believe that Adam and Eve marked the beginning, while others subscribe to the theory that we evolved from a quagmire of primordial soup, developed legs and learned how to make fire. I won't go back to the beginning of time, but this is my family story going back about four generations in a nutshell.

On the Squires' side, Thomas Squires was born in 1769. I don't know where he came from, but I do know he passed away in 1865 in North Carolina. My guess would be that he was from Scotland, considering red hair runs in our family and the surname "Squires" originates from Great Britain. His son was Thomas II, that subsequently had a son named James, my great-grandfather. James's son, George, was my grandfather. I never had the opportunity to meet my dad's parents; Grandma Veloney passed away when my dad was about ten. Grandpa George Houston Squires, was born in 1884 and worked as a blacksmith. He passed away in 1952 while my dad was in the military. Since dad's mom passed when he was young and his dad lived in a very small one-room house, my Uncle York and his wife Ruth helped raise my dad. They had a daughter, my cousin Doris, my dad said was like his sister. Uncle York was my dad's hero and roll model. York had joined the army and participated in the D-Day Invasion; I believe landing on Omaha Beach. After that he pushed into Germany and was a machine gunner in the Battle of the Bulge, eventually helping free Europe from the Nazis. York was a great all-around gentleman that passed away about a week before he was to turn ninety-nine, a true American hero. Most of the Squires family grew up and lived in a small town called Efland, North Carolina. It currently has a population of 734. It was definitely a rougher life when my dad was growing up back then; there were no Starbucks, you had to chop wood for heat and I believe you had to visit the local barber to have a tooth extracted.

My mom's side were the Bernreuter's. George Paulus Bernreuter came from Bayreuth, Germany. In 1841 he embarked on a journey across the Atlantic and then traveled over land, eventually settling in Illinois near East St. Louis. His son, my great-grandfather, was known as Big Joe. Joe had a son named George, my grandfather, who was born in 1897. Yes, both of my grandfathers were named George, which explains the origin of my name. If you were to consult Webster's Dictionary for the word "grandma" you would see an image of Grandma Hilma with a plate of freshly baked cookies in her hands. She was always full of smiles and would discreetly slip a dollar or some loose change into my pocket when we visited.

George and Hilma experienced the challenges of the Great Depression, which meant eating an apple down to three seeds and fishing in the creek for dinner. I loved playing at their old Victorian house, built in 1903 with a big wrap around front porch and a red barn in the back. George worked for the railroad so when the Depression hit, he didn't lose his job. They saved their pennies and paid $2,500 cash for the house in 1935, which was a significant amount of money at that time. It still has a horse hitching post in front and I always try to visit it when I'm in the area. A Norman Rockwell painting if there ever was one.

Given that my parents were educated and pragmatic planners, I'm inclined to believe that I was a well-planned baby, a fact that my mom recently confirmed. Dad was a high school dropout who obtained a GED during his service in the Air Force, then went on to earn an EdD in Education from Missouri State University in Columbia. Mom became a teacher who had earned multiple Master's degrees in Music, Math and English. A remarkable achievement, especially for a woman back then.

So, how did I end up being born in Arizona? My dad had developed respiratory problems, a spot on his lungs that was later removed. He said that if the X-ray machine at the Air Force induction center hadn't broken down on that fateful day when enlisted and they had detected the problem with his lung, he wouldn't have been accepted. Consequently, he would have never met my mom and I would never have come into existence. Guess I'm a lucky guy. Years later, a doctor told him that if he wanted to live a long life he should "venture westward young man, to a drier climate." So, they packed up their few belongings and headed west. My mom hated Arizona; it was dry, dusty, lacking distinct seasons and was far from her family. However, she loved my dad, so she acquiesced.

Growing Up

Dad had a passion for aviation and was a private pilot. One of his dreams was to become a commercial pilot, but he was color blind which doesn't work well if you're trying to land a plane using red and green runway landing lights or picking out a tie that matches your jacket. I remember flying with him when I was growing up…I believe I was in a plane before I could walk. Also, one of my earliest memories was watching Popeye on a small black-and-white television set. I was probably two or three years old. It had a rabbit ear antenna that allowed you to pick up 3 ½ stations. I guess that's why my mom would feed me nasty tasting spinach when I woke up after having a bad dream, just living the American dream.

Since my parents were educators, they believed in verbal communication and correction rather than corporal punishment. A good whack may have been better at times to drive a point home, but I skated by for the most part.

I do remember getting my first spanking; there were only two in my life. When I was about four, I encountered a group of older kids and they pulled me in my wagon a few of miles into the desert, let's go explore the world. They wanted me to pull them back, but I was too small, so after refusing they abandoned me and I never saw them again. Hopefully they were eaten by coyotes, bitten by rattlesnakes or experienced some other unfortunate event as payback for abandoning a small kid in the hot Arizona desert. I was gone most of the day prompting my parents to organize a search and comb the desert for me. My dad even flew around in his plane looking for me. When I arrived home, they weren't happy and that's when I received my first spanking. It was very traumatizing. I bet Lewis and Clark or Columbus never got punished for wandering off...I mean exploring.

The second time occurred during a visit to my Aunt Ruth's and Uncle Bob's. Bob owned a magnificent Austin Healey; it was his pride and joy. He allowed my mom to take it to pick up some fast food at the local drive-in, I believe it was "Dog N Suds." While returning, I took out a chocolate milkshake, my mom immediately told me not to open it. My hearing is fine, but my ability to follow directions and comply was lacking. Well, you can imagine how sixteen ounces of creamy, chocolate liquid looks on new carpet and seats. I considered this a learning moment; they didn't see it that way. Later in life, I would get into more trouble. My mom attributed it to my upbringing and being in a broken home. But I believe it was due to my innate curiosity, high level of activity and healthy sense of adventure.

My dad would attach cardboard wings to my arms and told me that if I ran fast enough, I could fly. What a great way to wear-out a kid. We were always working in his shop, building planes, cars and boats out of scraps of wood. The little things parents do and say no matter how small can last a lifetime. Case in point, we were at the movies one day and I told my dad that I could lie about my age to get in cheaper. Without hesitation, he said, "*It doesn't matter what they believe; it's what we know.*" This was a life lesson that probably never crossed his mind, but it had a lasting impression on me especially when I was raising my kids.

I loved to draw so when we had spelling tests at school, I preferred to draw a KAT rather than spell it. You could say I was developing my artistic abilities, which would help me later in life. Also, my parents told me that from a young age that I always wanted to knock on doors, no matter where we were to see if anyone was interested in playing. Ending up in sales, I basically did that for a living. It's called cold calling and I was quite proficient at it.

Due to my November birthday I was always one of the youngest kids in my class. When I enrolled in a new school, I was placed in second grade instead of third, even though I had completed second grade the previous year. After a couple of weeks and an IQ test, I was moved back to the third grade. I had a higher IQ before hitting my head so many times later in life. Also, when I was growing up, I experienced speech issues and received speech therapy several times a week. I had difficulty pronouncing my "S" and "Sh's." I still struggle with articulating "Sally at the seashore selling seashells." When I travel to another country, I can pick up some basic words. But then I'm reminded that I still need to continue working on being proficient in English before I move on to a secondary language.

I was a curious little juvenile. At the age of about eight, I broke into a construction shed with a friend. The police showed up, took me into custody and my mom had to come down to the station to retrieve me. That marked the start of my life of crime. Other than that, I was a model citizen in my early years.

In 1966, my brother Paul was born. He was a little white baby with red hair. He would observe all of my missteps, screw-ups and mistakes, and then for the most part avoid them. I consider myself a good role model in a twisted, paradoxical, reverse way.

Big Changes and Moving

In 1969, when I was nine years old, our life was significantly transformed. My parents went through a divorce. Years later, my dad confided in me that he had loved my mom; he described her as smart, intelligent and honest. However, he later fell in love with Carol. I'm sure it was a very messy time with a lot of painful moments. I know hurting my mom was a big regret, but sometimes life is unfair and as he once said; there are no do-overs for some decisions you make in your life. My mom packed up Paul and me then we headed back to St. Louis to be with family and experience all four seasons.

Upon our arrival, we stayed with my mom's sister, Jean, her husband Duane, and my cousins Veronica and Mark. In July of that year, I remember sitting in their living room and watching the first moon landing. Neil Armstrong stepping on the moon was like America winning the World Series, Superbowl and World Cup all at the same time, it was exciting! My cousin, Veronica, ended up becoming a teacher and Mark became a musician. Eventually, we moved to Berkeley, Missouri, closer to my mom's new teaching job.

York, Grandpa George, Grandma Veloney and Carl the day before York went into the Army

Carl Squires in Grade School

York Squires in Germany

Grandpa George's House painted by Doris

Carl Squires in the Air Force

George Houston Squires

George Houston Squires, the boy with the bat about 14 years old

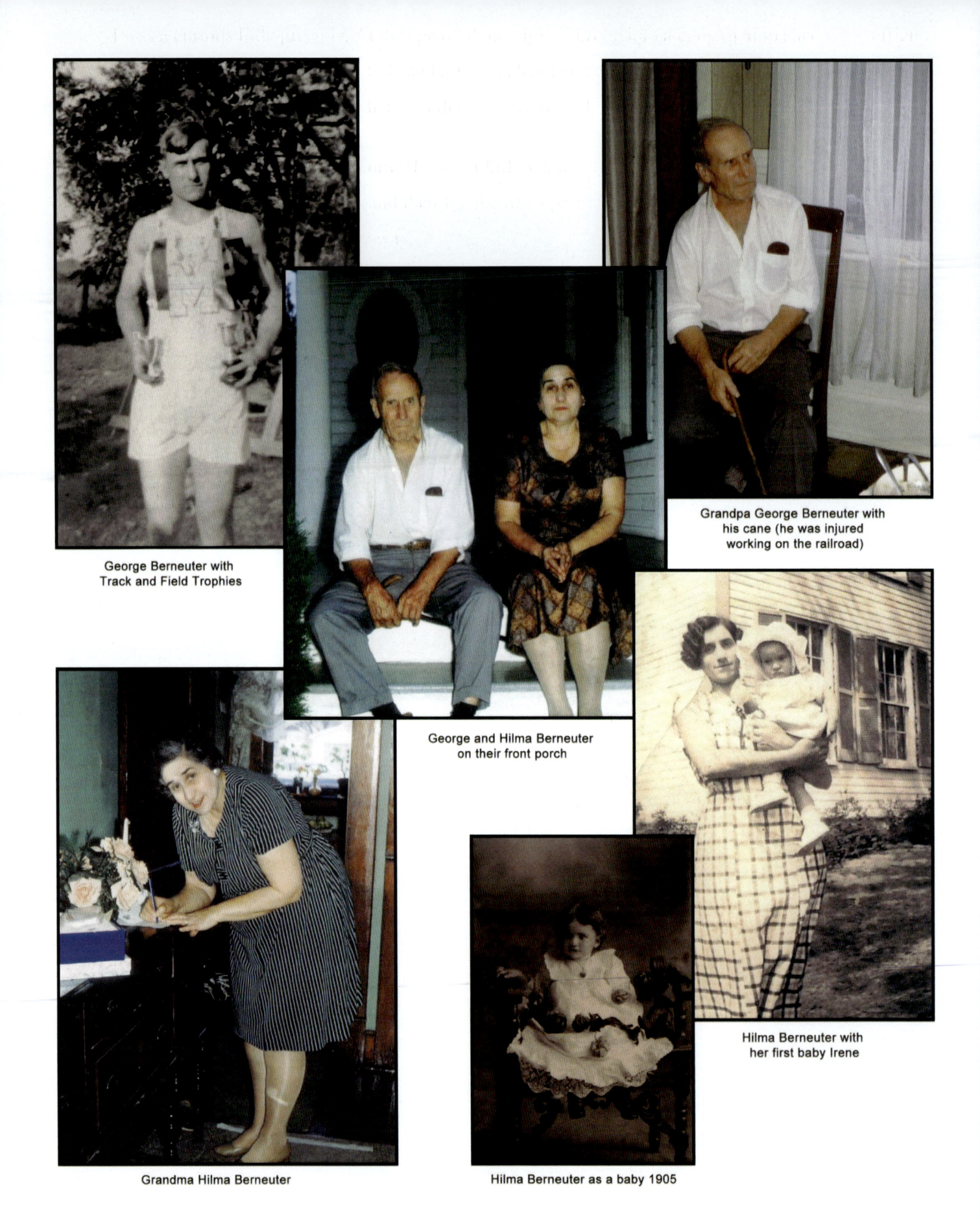

George Berneuter with
Track and Field Trophies

George and Hilma Berneuter
on their front porch

Grandpa George Berneuter with
his cane (he was injured
working on the railroad)

Hilma Berneuter with
her first baby Irene

Grandma Hilma Berneuter

Hilma Berneuter as a baby 1905

Irene and Carl

Irene Berneuter in High School

Carl Squires

Squires Family Christmas 1963

Irene Squires

George and his Exploring Wagon

York, Carl, George and Doris about 2020

George Squires with a boat we built out of wood scraps

Carl Squires Graduating from College the first in his family to do so!

216 West Adams Street, O'Fallon IL, built in 1903, purchased in 1935 with a red barn and if you look close you can see the old horse hitching post

Carl Squires and his plane at Sky Harbor Airport AZ

Irene and George 1962

George Squires
in Kindergarden

Christmas picture taken at the Mall,
Santa brought me a race car track
that my Dad worked most of
the night putting together
(Santa doesn't look happy,
I guess it's not your dream job)

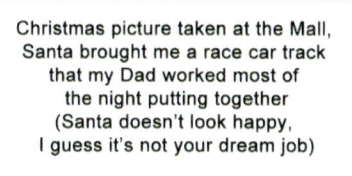

George and Paul 1969

George and Paul 1966

Cousin Veronica, Mark, Paul and George

Chapter 2

The 70's - Big Trouble and Then Some

DAD CAME BACK TO VISIT US IN ST. LOUIS A COUPLE OF TIMES A YEAR and we would also travel to Arizona occasionally. We moved into an apartment in Berkeley; embarking on our Midwest life, enjoying all the seasons…hot, muggy, rainy, cold, cloudy and sometimes sunny. I recall one of our neighbors was Bobby Tolan, a professional baseball player for the St. Louis Cardinals. Baseball players didn't have big paydays at that time like they do today. Then there was a guy with a pet monkey and another guy that owned a Ford Shelby Cobra. What a cool car! I thought someday I'm going to have something that spectacular... and maybe even a monkey.

But for now, since I was only eleven years old, my dream was a red Colt minibike from Sears with a 3 1/2 horsepower lawnmower engine, pull rope to start it, no shocks and only one rear drum brake…the emergency brake was dragging your feet. After months of begging and pleading I finally wore my mom down and got it! The first time I rode the minibike I flipped off over a dirt berm, resulting in a sizeable bump on the back of my head. I never told my mom, but I did appropriate an old football helmet and started wearing it. Everything was going great. I was making new friends, joined Cub Scouts and had a purple Schwinn Stingray bicycle with a three-speed mid stick shifter, ape hanger handlebars and a banana seat, one styling ride. I would cruise around on it collecting empty soda bottles to redeem for minibike gasoline. By the way, gas was only 26 cents per gallon back then.

One time my mom went on a date and left Paul and me with a babysitter at our apartment. Well, I wasn't fond of her and being a curious young lad, I wondered how the container of pepper spray that I found worked. According to her reaction I wouldn't recommend using it as air freshener.

Another Move

My mom started dating a guy named Harold. Before I knew it, they were married and we moved into his house with his two daughters. For a short time, all was well. However, as with many blended families with young children there were a lot of moving parts and things started to go awry quickly. One upside was that the older daughter, Jan introduced me to Rock'n'Roll. She was a mess, but had good taste in music; the Rolling Stones, Don McLean, Jimi Hendrix and Elton John. A year later when I picked up an old record player my first two albums were Elton John's *Yellow Brick Road* and *Led Zeppelin II.* Also, while I lived there, I joined another Boy Scout troop, but I was an outsider to them. During the second meeting, I disagreed with some of their game rules and ended getting into an altercation with a couple of the Scouts, which didn't go over well. By the way, I'm a great team player as long as people do things my way. They started chasing me down the street when I ran into some older kids and asked for help. After quickly explaining why I was fleeing from a pack of Scouts, which they found funny, they agreed to help and delayed the pack, thus allowing me to escape. That was the end of my Boy Scout career.

Another bright idea I had was to have a barbecue at a local park about a half mile down the road called Dunegant. What do you need for a barbecue? Hot dogs, combustible materials and accelerant; there were hot dogs in the refrigerator and plenty of dead wood at the park. But I couldn't find any lighter fluid around the house, so I put half a gallon of regular leaded gasoline in a milk jug. That should do the trick or maybe a whole gallon would be better. Little did I know at that time gas was much more flammable than BBQ lighter fluid. After I started the fire, I went to pour more gasoline on it and the flames quickly came back into the jug. I immediately threw it down causing fire to spread to the dry brush in the area, resulting in a couple of acres going up in flames. What can I say? Oops! Lesson learned; no more BBQing with gasoline. There was a book called *ON FIRE* by John O'Leary that my brother turned me on to. It's about a nine-year-old boy who had a similar incident and ended up with third-degree burns on 87% of his body. A great book about survival and motivation. Just imagining what could have happened and how close I was to engulfing myself in flames scared me then and still scares me now. The first two things I want to avoid, given a choice are burning or falling to my death…they just give you too much time to think. If I had 9 lives like a cat, that would definitely be number 1. Shortly thereafter, the marriage fell apart and we moved back to Berkeley, settling in a ranch-style house on Cadillac Lane with a spacious yard and radiant heated floors.

New Neighborhood and I do Mean Hood

The house was great, but the neighborhood and school system were starting to decline. Many people from Kinloch, the predominantly Black neighboring community, were relocating to Berkeley. The white population started panicking and many people started moving out, then the property values began to plummet. The city council even enacted a law prohibiting the placement of "FOR SALE" signs in front yards due to the excessive number of them. The demographics of Berkeley today show that 96.4% of the population is African American, while 1.8% is white, reflecting a 47% decrease in the overall population since 1980. So went the great white flight out of that area.

Berkeley was quickly becoming a challenging area. I was a thirteen-year-old, 98-pound kid who was a minority at the local junior high. About that time, my mom enrolled me in Fred Wren's Taekwondo school of martial arts to keep me busy and introduce some structure into my life. I participated in a couple of tournaments and was a decent student earning a Green Belt, which is three ranks below Black Belt.

At the junior high school there was a kid named Montes who was the quarterback of the Junior Varsity football team. He was about 30 pounds heavier and 2 inches taller than me. For some reason, he wasn't a fan of mine. One day as I was leaving class, Montes cornered me and hit me causing all my books to fall. When trapped in a corner, you have two options; fight or take a beating. The first option just seemed better. Since he was bigger than me, I knew I had to take him down so first I kicked out his knee, causing him to drop to the ground, which surprised him. Overwhelmed with fear and afraid at that point he would get up and kill me, I started hitting him until he lost consciousness. I looked pretty good in the end, but him not so much, in boxing I believe they call it a Knock Out. After being dragged to the school office and explaining that it was purely self-defense, I was still suspended. To me it was a proportional response to an unprovoked attack, but they said based on his injuries it didn't look like self-defense. When I returned to school I thought, "I'm in a world of hurt." So, I purchased a knife from the nearby hardware store and strapped it to my leg under my pants for protection. Turns out Montes and all his buddies were so freaked out by me, the crazy little kid, I was never touched again by anybody.

As a young kid, about twelve years old, I remember slipping out of my bedroom window and meeting friends late at night. I can't believe most kids haven't done that at least once, so be easy on me. One time we converged at Ferguson Middle School; we weren't up to any nefarious activities but it was just cool to hang out after curfew. While we were walking through the school yard when several cop cars lit us up, so we all took off in different directions. I ran down to a park called January-Walbash and dove under a bush, a safe place, they would never find me…just lay low and be quiet.

After about twenty minutes I saw flash lights combing the brush…then in front of me two polished black shoes appeared. We hadn't done anything bad, but if they grabbed me it would be a trip down to the police station and a call to my mom to retrieve me for being a minor out after curfew, so I took off running like a cat from a bath. I could feel hands grabbing at my back and shirt which just made me press my internal gas petal down harder. I was running through an open field next to the park, most houses in Missouri don't have fenced yards unlike California. The key word here is most…as I ran, I hit a chain link fence, I was running so hard I flipped over it and to my amazement landed on my feet. An effective but painful way to gain ground on my pursuer. Well most homeowners don't just put up a fence just on one side of their yard, if you want to contain a dog you do both sides and the back. I hit the other side at full speed and flipped again landing on my feet, Olympic gold! Now I had some ground between me and the cop so I headed into a housing subdivision, then slipped under a truck to hide. Minutes later I saw flashlights and shoes coming up to the truck and pulled myself up into the engine compartment. They didn't see me and moved on. I waited there until sunrise then strolled back to my house, climbed back in my bedroom window and all was good. I didn't always escape, there were other times that I wasn't so lucky…as you will soon read about.

The Next Move East Side

Shortly thereafter we moved to Wood River, Illinois. I think my mom believed the area would be good for Paul and me, but my new friends quickly disproved that assumption. The Wood River/Roxana area was known for its oil refineries, making it a dirty, smelly place. I remember washing a black film off my face every night with rubbing alcohol. The EPA must have overlooked that city for years. The football team was even named "the Shells" after the oil company. Lawsuits were filed years later by people who had become ill and passed away after being exposed to toxic chemicals, such as benzene products that were being released into the air, soil and groundwater. In 1986, the Shell refinery leaked over 9,000 gallons of benzene into the groundwater. Even after the cleanup, a fifty-foot test hole revealed 260,000 times the safe allowable limit of chemicals in the groundwater. Anyway, with my new friends I was not getting on a better track, quite the opposite.

I had traded my minibike for a fast racing go-kart that was equipped with a two-stroke 125cc McCulloch engine, essentially an oversized chainsaw motor that could reach speeds of 60 mph. At four inches off the ground it felt like you were driving an Indy car. We would load the go-kart into the huge trunk of my mom's 1969 Gold Fury III, with half of it hanging out and go to a closed department store parking lot. Most stores were closed on Sundays due to the Bible Belt's Blue Laws, observing the Lord's day of rest. One fateful day, I was speeding around a corner at full throttle when I hit a concrete parking/planter curb hard. The magnesium rims exploded, the one-inch solid axle bent, the cart flew up a few feet in the air and the frame cracked in half. I had no helmet and little common sense at that time. My short life flashed before my eyes; it could have been the end of me. Definitely, it was the end of the go-kart. Life number 2 of my 9 lives.

One very positive thing I did in Wood River was to learn how to work on machines. I had always been one of those kids that would take things apart to try to understand how stuff worked. We would build and modify bikes so they would be able to jump the ramps that we built, Evil Knievel stuff. Also, I would tear apart the go-cart engine after every two or three times we ran it to replace piston rings, torque bolts down and clean the carburetor. It was a good way to stay out of trouble and learn about machines. I still enjoy doing those kinds of things today.

Just like other normal kids growing up we had pet alligators and snakes. I think my mom believed that a dog required just too much maintenance. Later in life Jenny would want a dog, but I didn't. In any successful marriage it is essential to understand that you need to compromise, meeting in the middle and working things out are key. So, we got a dog, Dexter. He's great, but he requires a lot of work. Growing up we did have a Siamese cat that we found named Kitty, that cat hung around with my mom for about twenty years.

I ended up falling into or I should say choosing, a bad crowd to hang out with. As the new kid in the neighborhood, I found it was always easier to fit in with troubled kids rather than the scholars or jocks. That's when I started smoking pot and drinking, among other things. I'll be the first to admit that at that point in my life, I was not making good decisions. Real stupid risks, stupid friends, stupid me. When I was writing this book, I took the time to research some of my old acquaintances, a few of them are in prison or have since passed. Certainly not the kind of crowd that went to Harvard or Yale. By the way, it's important to note that being intelligent and having common sense are two totally different things.

I was arrested several times, for various offenses ranging from smoking pot in a public park and shoplifting, to breaking into the high school on a cold night when I needed shelter from the weather. One time, I was picked up and the cops took me to the Wood River Police Station. At that time, Tom's mom (Tom, was my future partner in crime), was working there and knew me. Instead of putting me in a holding cell, she was nice enough to let me sit next to her at her desk. As I sat there, my reptilian brain kicked in. I saw people coming and going through the card-keyed secured door about 15 feet away. All of a sudden when someone came through the door, I jumped up and in the blink of an eye, I bolted through it. Keep in mind they knew who I was and where I lived, but I just wanted to leave that joint and wasn't thinking more than ten minutes ahead…if that. The Fire Department was located next to the police station, so when I looked behind me there were a half dozen police officers and just as many firefighters chasing me. I was making good time and gaining ground. Usain Bolt set the 100-meter record at 9.58 seconds in the 2009 World Championships. I think I was going a little faster than that. I turned left down an alley and quickly discovered it was a dead end. After that, they escorted me back to the station, it looked like a parade with me as the Grand Marshal and then they locked me up. I guess "A" for effort, "F" for planning.

As I already shared, I managed to escape a few times, but I was caught and taken to Juvenile Hall on several occasions. I guess that's where I learned that no matter what keeping your mouth shut is crucial. Talking can only make things worse.

A Really Bad Decision

On Halloween night in 1974, I attended the KISS Rock'n'Roll concert at Keil Auditorium in St. Louis. As an enterprising individual, I decided to make some money by bringing some drugs along with a loaded .22 revolver pistol for protection. As I walked through the security gates, a half dozen security guards and police officers drew their weapons. Think of the last scene in *Butch Cassidy and the Sundance Kid,* with guns blazing and bullets flying. I knew I didn't have a chance, so I just put my hands up.

They took me to the St. Louis City Jail, the next day my dad came in and somehow convinced them to let me go. He told them that I was from "good stock" and promised to take me away so they would never see me again. I have to give it to my dad; he was a good negotiator and saved me that time. We drove back to Wood River, where I packed up my belongings. That was the first and only time I saw my dad break down and cry. He was taking me away from my mom, but there were no other options at that point.

North Carolina Here I Come

My dad was attending school in Columbia, Missouri for his doctorate in education, so I went there for a little while. I continued to seek out an assortment of drugs, marijuana and surrounded myself with bad friends, still heading down a troubled path full of potholes. A few months later my dad was hired by Central Piedmont Community College in Charlotte as an administrator. Since he grew up in North Carolina I believe that's where he finally wanted to settle down. Shortly thereafter he started buying land to build Carol and his dream home in the country.

In North Carolina the first thing I had to do of course was to find some new troubled friends. I was also bused to an intercity for school in the name of racial diversity, under the Brown vs. the Board of Education ruling, which didn't help stabilize my situation. I developed a "style" consisting of an old army trench coat, black boots and long hair. I guess if I wanted to be a troublemaking hippie, I had to look like one.

During the next few months, I helped my dad clear a road for his new house. Nothing screams safety like entrusting a young kid in the middle of the forest with a chainsaw and an axe. My dad probably thought I might dismember myself, but at least I would stay out of trouble. But I've found that if you're creative, have a good imagination and willing to work hard you can always find trouble. I quickly learned how to hotwire my dad's prized, fully restored 1962 Willys Jeep with two wires attached to alligator clips and I would go out joyriding. One day, my dad and Carol passed me on the road driving in the opposite direction. There weren't many old Army jeeps on the road, so I was easy to spot; the game was up. When I arrived home, my dad was sitting at the kitchen table waiting for me. In no uncertain terms he proceeded to draw a flowchart, with me represented as a triangle, the jeep as a circle and my room as a square. In graphic detail, he illustrated with additional lines and X's, connecting me to my room and negating the Jeep, that I was grounded and no longer allowed to use the Jeep. I bet very few people misunderstood my dad; he was a good communicator. Later in life we would look back and laugh at it, but not at that time. I still ended up getting into more legal, school and friend trouble. By the way, my dad never "lost it" or got really upset, no matter what I did. Years later, I asked him how he managed to stay calm, he told me the key was to *always believe in your kids.* " I believe in my kids, but I'm relieved they never really put me to the test.

May I also add Carol was always very supportive. If I were her there are several times that I would've wanted to leave me tied up on some dark country road, but she always hung in there and I think she believed there was light at the end of the tunnel. So, thank you Carol!

Exodus

It came to a point where I had had enough of North Carolina and North Carolina probably had enough of me. So, I put on a half dozen layers of clothes, it was easier than carrying a suitcase. Then I walked out to the highway and hitchhiked 716 miles back to Missouri. Unlike today, you could hitchhike and jump trains without getting cut up by a serial killer. Still a long way for a young kid with just a few dollars in his pocket. The "run-away" note that I recently found in an old box that my dad and mom saved said:

I'm leaving because I feel like a prisoner & I don't like moving here and then moving again in 3 months. I know if they catch me, I will be in trouble so I will try to get a job and stay out of trouble. I will be ok. George

I recently went to North Carolina to help my stepmother; Carol move after my dad passed away. While driving to the Charlotte airport to catch a flight home I saw a young kid, probably seventeen or eighteen years old. He was on the corner of the highway exit ramp with a sign, "HUNGRY - NEED MONEY PLEASE." I thought about my situation fifty years ago and handed him a twenty dollar bill out the window, I hope he finds his way.

I finally arrived back in Missouri and had nowhere to go. Believe it or not my teenage brain wasn't thinking that far ahead at that time. It was winter and it was really cold. I stumbled upon an old unlocked dump truck at a construction site where I would sleep with my layers of clothes on and then leave before the workers arrived in the morning. Sometimes my dinner came from a McDonald's dumpster; by the way, the Big Macs still taste the same. It really makes you appreciate a warm bed and a good meal.

My dad had put together and distributed a recent picture of me. I had long hair and was wearing my army trench coat. The back of the picture contained information with my name, age and contact numbers for my dad, mom and probation officer. Finally, the police caught up with me and contacted my mom and dad. They were of course afraid I'd take off again if they brought me home and also believed I needed some professional help at that point. One option was to place me in a secured rehabilitation facility with other troubled kids in St. Louis. After being placed there and still being that enterprising individual, I contacted my friends and shared with them that I had a captive market. If they could provide me with some marijuana, we could make a few bucks. Unfortunately, the administration at the rehabilitation center didn't approve of the idea. Once they found out about it, they quickly asked me to leave.

By then, my mom had come to the conclusion that Wood River was not a good place for my brother or me, so she moved to a nice neighborhood in West St. Louis called Creve Coeur. Definitely a big step up from Wood River or Berkeley. Just by coincidence, Tom's parents moved from Wood River to Creve Coeur around the same time. This was great. I had a friend in a new up-and-coming area, a place where people had money and nice houses. It didn't take long before Tom and I figured out that all these kids with money spelled opportunity.

The Next Opportunity

With our connections and resources, we decided to start a business. Before you judge me, remember marijuana is basically legal today. I considered our actions illegal, but not immoral. In 1978, marijuana was classified as a Class 1 drug, similar to heroin, which seemed crazy to me. Jerome was our supplier and he was connected to an organization known as "The Company," which transported marijuana from Florida to Illinois. Let's fast forward for a minute; after I left the business this is what happened to them;

The Chicago Tribune published this on February 6, 1986

MARIJUANA SMUGGLER PLEADS GUILTY 44 TIMES

Richard Dial Thorp, former head of "The Company" a marijuana smuggling ring that has been called the biggest ever in the U.S. has pleaded guilty to 44 criminal counts in federal court.

Thorp faces up to 303 years imprisonment or life without parole and fines up to $945,000.

The Company allegedly smuggled about 900 tons of Colombian marijuana worth about $55 million dollars. At its height, the group operated a fleet of cargo planes and trucks and airfields throughout Illinois and Missouri.

Thorp had eluded police since 1979 when he fled from a Georgia drug trial. He was arrested under an assumed name in Florida in 1982...

We would go to Illinois once or twice a week to pick up marijuana. At first, we used Tom's purple AMC Gremlin which didn't have a trunk. Tom was a little older than me and had landed a job in his dad's mailroom. To conceal the marijuana, we would stash it in large mail bags from his work, then padlock them just in case we were pulled over by the police. I believe tampering with mail is a federal crime, but what's another few years' in prison at that point? We felt it was worth the risk. I would recruit friends from school, such as Rich and Steve along with other willing volunteers to come over to my house where we would break up the bales of marijuana and then repackage it for sale. Over the next year, we established a reliable and profitable distribution network. Of course, my mom, being a smart woman, figured out what I was doing and told me that I'd have to stop or move out. By that time, I believe I was making more money than she was, thousands a month, so I decided to move out and continue my business endeavors.

Between the time I moved to Creve Coeur and moved out of my mom's house my girlfriend, Becky, set fire to my mom's Ross Ridge condo. Rich, Becky and I had left to play Frisbee outside, we returned about thirty or forty minutes later and the condo was filled with smoke. Initially, I thought Paul was burning something in the kitchen. However, when I opened my bedroom door flames leaped out. I ran into the kitchen, grabbed every large pot we had then placed them under all the bathtub faucets. I wrapped a wet towel around my mouth and nose then proceeded to run up and down the stairs, throwing water on the fire. I asked Rich to help, he looked at me and said, "you're going to die," then ran out. It was probably the wise thing to do. I figured I had nothing to lose; if the fire didn't kill me, my mom would. I lost most of my clothes, stereo, bed, some cool 4'x 8' murals of Led Zeppelin and the band YES that I had hand-painted, and the condo had major smoke damage. It was caused by a cigarette that Becky thought she had extinguished before putting it into her purse. When my mom arrived home, the fire department was just packing up and there was a pile of burnt furniture in the front yard. Remember what I said about my dad always staying calm? Well, that didn't always apply to my mom.

Another very difficult story to share, but as I mentioned in my introduction, I'm striving to be open and truthful, so here goes. While living with my mom I acquired some pills, specifically barbiturates. I didn't know how strong they were and took a couple in school one day. They turned out to be stronger than I had anticipated, and I was sent home. This was bad. My parents always held education in very high regard, so failing in school in my mind was worse than robbing a bank or stealing a police car. I was concerned that the school would contact my mom and there would be consequences. So, I figured that I'd take a few more pills to numb myself before I had to face her. Let me just say this before you do, that was really stupid. I ended up passing out. Rich came over to my house and found the front door unlocked, so he went up to my room. It wasn't a pretty sight. He took me to the hospital and they had to pump my stomach to save me. The next day, I woke up with tubes in every part of my body. I just wanted to numb the pain because of how badly I had messed up. To say that was a stupid teenage move would be an understatement. My mom deserves sainthood for still believing in me after all the things I put her through. I will never be able to repay her for her love and for not disowning me. Life number 3 of my 9 lives.

As far as moving out, Tom and I ended up getting an apartment to live in and conducted business out of another. In our main apartment we had a sunken living room, new stylish furniture and a stereo system that would make the Rolling Stones proud. With a few thousand watts, eight bass speakers, four mid-range speakers and four dome tweeters, it could make a chandelier shake and swing two floors up. Tom picked up a new Camaro, while I went old school with a 1967 Firebird. It had a beautiful custom pearl white paint job, a top-of-the-line Pioneer Super Tuner stereo and chrome Craiger rims. At the end of that business venture, we had so much money that we would weigh it; it was easier than counting. By the way, if you ever need to know what a $20 bill weights it's one gram. 454 of them equals one pound, $9,080 dollars.

Oh Boy, I'm in Big Trouble…! Continued

Everything was rolling right along until one day Curt, one of our associates, told me that he had been working with a couple of guys for the past year. They were interested in pursuing bigger opportunities and had expressed a desire to meet me. Well, I finally agreed, even though I was always suspicious of any new business partners. These guys had my radar on full alert, but Curt kept assuring me that they were ok.

As page one of my story begins, I met Curt's "friends" and then we drove to our second apartment where I had the marijuana. On the way over, we took separate cars. I picked up a gun that I had stashed at a neighbor's house because as I shared, there was something just unsettling about these new guys. One thing I've learned in life is to *trust your intuition; there are always reasons why you feel a certain way.*

Curt and the two other guys arrived at the apartment. Shortly thereafter, money was brought out and chaos ensued. I won't rehash what I've already told you. The police released me and followed me for about a week until they realized I wasn't going to lead them to anyone or anywhere. Soon after, they issued a warrant for my arrest.

I turned myself in and went to the St. Louis County Jail, where I spent thirty-two days. Even though I had the financial resources to get out, Ben my attorney, said the court would want some punishment and giving them a little jail time was a good strategy. It wasn't too bad, but it wasn't too good either. I read a lot of books, additionally I did a few jailhouse tattoos using a needle and ink from a Bic pen for my newly incarcerated friends. I've always been a pretty good artist, so I had value and nobody messed with me, with one exception. There was a guy nicknamed "Muscles," he was twice my size and I believe it wouldn't have been a good idea to make jokes about his Mama. One day, he approached me while I had a Snickers bar in my hand and wanted it. Of course, I like Snickers and I still do, so I said NO. Next thing I know I'm on the floor, still holding the Snickers. At that point I thought it was in my best interest to graciously let the big, overdeveloped gentleman have what he asked for. Later that week he was jumped by some other guys whom he had also bullied and ended up in solitary confinement, ensuring that he would not be a problem again.

I remember when the kids were teenagers, we took a cruise along the Inside Passage from Alaska to Vancouver. There was my mom, Bob, Veronica, Rick, Kent, Don and a few more family members. We started in Anchorage, then went to Glacier Bay, rented canoes in Juneau and ziplined in Skagway. It was beautiful. One night at dinner on the ship someone raised a question, sort of a challenge. What was the best meal you have ever had in your life? As we went around the table someone said Lobster in Manie, while another was Wagyu steak in Japan, everyone shared their mouthwatering stories. But I won; it went something like this…"I saw the McDonald's as I walked out the door, it was less than a half block down the street and that was my first stop after spending thirty-two days eating some of the worst food on earth in the St. Louis County Jail. Big Mac here I come, it was fantastic!" Sometimes the situation dictates the quality of the experience.

When my trial arrived, Ben assured me that I had nothing to worry about. He said he knew the prosecuting attorney and they had gone to school together. I hesitantly believed him. As I stood in front of the judge, my charges were read; possession of over 1 ounce of marijuana and carrying a concealed weapon. Essentially, it was as like I had a few marijuana cigarettes and a pocket knife. The judge then looked at me and asked, "Did you have 36 grams, 36 ounces, or 36 pounds?" To which I responded "Pounds, your Honor." Evidently, he had the police report in front of him. Then he looked at the prosecutor and asked, "Are you okay with this charge?" He replied, "Yes, your Honor." The judge reviewed the report again and asked me, "Was this a loaded gun?" Being an honest person, of course I replied "Yes, your Honor." He then glanced over at the prosecuting attorney and asked once more, "Are you sure you're okay with this?" The prosecutor affirmed "Yes, your Honor."

The prosecutor asked for time served along with five years of unsupervised probation, the judge hesitantly agreed. Ben was the best defense money could buy, at least until OJ was on trial. I was sentenced, but nothing stayed on my record since I was a minor at the time of the arrest. Dodged that bullet big time.

Ben retired on July 22, 2021. He was a great attorney and I've worked with a few, so thank you Jerome. The local newspaper that covered his last trial printed this.

EWARDSVILLE - It's not often a defense attorney gets a standing ovation when he disposes of a court case, but that's what happened when Ben Allen of Alton appeared for the last time on a case.

Circuit Judge Kyle Napp, after accepting the plea agreement at a recent court session, stood up and said, "Anyone who has been such a good lawyer and such a good man deserves a round of applause." It's not often a defense attorney gets a standing ovation when he disposes of a court case, but that's what happened when Ben Allen of Alton appeared for the last time on a case.

The case involved a man accused of unlawful use of a weapon for allegedly firing shots in the air. Allen explained in a recent interview that his client had shot into the air as a warning to some people, and he had no prior criminal record.

Allen worked out an agreement with a prosecutor to allow his client to serve a term of probation, with a provision for a reduction to a misdemeanor if he completes the probation requirements. The prison sentence would have been between 4 and 15 years.

"It was a fair outcome, and that's all I ever wanted was a fair outcome," Allen said. He has tried at least 100 murder cases and at least 1,000 total criminal cases.

Allen said between 90 and 95 percent of criminal defendants are good for the crimes of which they are accused, but his job has been to get the best outcome possible for his clients, who are entitled to a fair trial.

Veteran Assistant State's Attorney Susan Jensen said Allen is one of two lawyers she would hire if she ever got in trouble.

The police in the courtroom weren't happy and wanted to pin a drug bust on someone. I believe Curt ended up taking the fall for the drug charges that he was originally arrested for, which I found out that was the reason he set me up. A couple of years later, Curt was shot and killed by the police during another drug deal. This is from an article by the St. Louis Globe-Democrat newspaper:

Detective McPortland had just bought the tablets for $1,550. Moments after the transaction was completed, he pulled out his badge, drew his pistol, and identified himself as a county police officer. Curtis Stewart took one or two steps backward, pulled the pistol from his pocket, and pointed it at McPortland. McPortland fired once, striking Curtis Steward in the chest...he was pronounced dead at county hospital.

Trying to Fly Straight and Staying Alive

I had to drop out of high school the last semester of my senior year, it's challenging to attend classes while incarcerated in the county jail. If you hadn't noticed, I went to a lot of schools; my count was nine in twelve years. While I was never interested in attending my class reunion, still I valued education and was determined to graduate. I had a meeting with the Parkway North High School Vice Principal, Mr. Hugo; we had a few meetings before and I don't think he would have been my first choice for a character reference. I believe he was a good guy, he just didn't appreciate some of my activities in his school. I remember being very honest with him, at that point I didn't have anything to lose. He was very curious about how the drug business worked. I explained supply, demand, profit margins, distribution, evading the authorities and cash flow. Maybe next semester he would consider hiring me to teach a business class...that was probably a long shot. I just needed a quarter credit to graduate and he suggested taking Driver's Ed that summer.

The driving instructor quickly realized that I knew how to drive since I had been doing it for a couple of years and owned the nicest car in the parking lot. He was an older guy that just didn't want to get killed by a student driver prior to retirement. I was his go-to student when he wanted to relax in the car with a cup of coffee and read the newspaper. Just a little side note; when you go to the DMV to get your license for the first time, bring a licensed driver with you. A year before, I passed the driving test with flying colors. When the DMV tester asked me how I got there, I replied that I drove. This didn't go over well since I didn't have a license before passing the test. They wouldn't issue my license until I returned with another licensed driver. Also, they warned me that if I moved my car, they would call the police.

I passed Driver's Ed. With my last quarter credit in the books, I received my high school diploma in the mail that summer. Now, what do I do?

Tom continued his life of crime and making good money. However, I valued my freedom much more than money, so I decided to leave that outlaw life behind. Once you have your freedom taken away, I believe it gives you a new perspective on life. Simply put, an appreciation on being able to just walk out the door if you don't like were you are at. It's something you can read it in a book or watch a movie about, but it will never truly hit home unless it really happens to you. Rich was working at King Henry the VIII, doing room service and seemed to enjoy it. So, I applied for a job there and was hired. The pay and tips were okay, but as you can imagine my cash flow was greatly reduced, so I ended up moving back in with my mom. I sold my Firebird and bought a new red GS400 Suzuki motorcycle. It was my only form of transportation during the scorching summer and the freezing cold, snowy and icy Missouri winter that year.

Early one very cold morning, I was driving down a four-lane road called Natural Bridge, all bundled up. I wore jeans over long underwear, a flannel shirt, a sweatshirt, leather coat, heavy gloves and boots. It was so cold my visor was fogging up, making it hard to see. I had a full-coverage BELL helmet that I had bought less than thirty days before at the same time I picked up the motorcycle. I remember asking the salesperson "why I should buy a $100 BELL helmet when there were $25 helmets hanging on the next rack?" His answer was, "You have a $25 head, buy a $25 helmet." What a great sales pitch! I bought the BELL. Traffic was light that day and I was going about 60 mph when another car from the opposite direction approached me going about 50 mph. As it neared, everything seemed fine, but the next second the car crossed into my lane. Now let's do some simple math; 60 mph plus 50 mph, that's equivalent to hitting a stationary object at 110 mph. Even if you hit something at just 60 mph, physics dictates that you would travel, or in my case fly 88 feet in one second. I had no time to maneuver and hit the car head-on.

They say that when you have a near-death experience, time slows way down. Well, they're right. I remember vividly every microsecond when I hit the car. Later I discovered that it was registered to the Catholic Church and being driven by a sixty-five-year-old nun. In that slow-motion moment my thoughts were, "Oh my God, I'm dead." As I flew over the car, I made direct eye contact with the nun, her eyes were wide open in shock and then my inside voice said, "You bitch." Those were my exact thoughts, no editing. Hope God gives me a pass for that one based on the situation. I rocketed off the motorcycle and hit the road about 200+ feet later, then started rolling and sliding. If there were Olympic judges sitting on the side of the street watching, I believe I would have received a perfect score of 10-10-10. A second later, I stood up but then I thought it would be better to go back down in case anything was broken and started crawling over to the side of the road. One guy ran across the street and said, "I saw the whole thing, and you flew really far." Well, no kidding! Find a phone and call 911!

Shortly thereafter the ambulance and police arrived. The motorcycle was totaled with the front wheel pushed next to the motor. It had less than 700 miles on it. The car was also a mess, but unbelievably I was okay. I just had bruises where my legs had hit the handlebars as I launched over the car and the $100 BELL helmet was cracked in half right down the middle. Guess I need to thank that guy who sold me the helmet. Life number 4 of my 9 lives.

The church's insurance contacted me the next day. Of course, after they saw the car and the motorcycle, they thought this was going to be a significant lawsuit. They first asked how I was and then what I needed. I told them that I was okay, but I wanted a new motorcycle and helmet. The following day there was a man on my doorstep with a new red motorcycle, a BELL helmet and liability release paperwork. My mom thought I had learned my lesson, but evidently not. I still ride today.

I continued to work at King Henry's with Rich. Riding home in winter after working late on those bone chilling cold Missouri nights on a motorcycle was tough. One night I was heading home doing about 140 mph, that motorcycle had a tall sixth gear with a great top end, when I noticed red lights flashing behind me. As my exit ramp approached, I had already begun to slow down so I pulled over. The cop said he had been attempting to catch up to me for the past three miles. Then he asked why I was going so fast? I said it was cold and I wanted to get home. He said "you know the faster you go the colder it gets." My response was "you can only get so cold then it's a matter of just getting to someplace warm, my exit is a couple hundred feet away and I promise to do the speed limit." He took a minute to ponder what I said, I think I saw him grin, then he agreed that in an odd way it made sense and let me go. I really missed having a car that year.

Sometimes, on those cold nights instead of riding my motorcycle I would hitch a ride home with friends. One guy owned a 1966 Ford Fairlane hot rod with a 289 engine and he considered himself a bona fide race car driver. Driving home late one night we were on the back roads near Creve Coeur Park, speeding or should I say flying, when we unexpectedly reached a sharp corner...we didn't make it. There are houses there now, but back then there were just empty fields and telephone poles. The car hit a pole broadside and wrapped around it like a piece of wet pasta. I was in the back seat without a seat belt; safety first was not my motto at that time. I went flying out of the side window as if I had been shot out of a cannon. Next thing I recall was lying in a dark field with so much blood pouring out of my head I couldn't see. The cut on my forehead, above my right eye was over two inches long and went deep into my skull. The other guys had various injuries; broken arm, collarbone and leg. When I arrived at the hospital, they cleaned me up and suggested that I wait until morning to see a plastic surgeon. Sure, glad I waited because that Frankenstein look wouldn't have been good later in life. Inner and outer stitches totaled fifty. I settled with the insurance for doctor bills and $2,500, which wasn't much considering the injuries. Life number 5 of my 9 lives.

Later that year, I was riding my second red GS400 Suzuki motorcycle down a highway ramp, going a little too fast and accidentally clipped a car, causing me to bounce off like a pinball and bending the frame of the motorcycle. If I had hit two feet farther to the right, I would only have one foot and a permanent lean. I sold the GS400 engine because the rest of the bike was beyond repair. Then I purchased a new GS750L Suzuki, which turned out to be a great bike that I enjoyed for the next ten years.

New Job, New Views, New Trouble

I was hanging out at Tom's house one day when a guy mentioned that a company called Carborundum was hiring. They worked on the sewer systems, which didn't excite me. What did excite me was the fact that they were paying $10.75 per hour, while the minimum wage was only $2.65. To put that in today's perspective, a dollar in 1979 is equal to $4.14 in 2024, which means it was equivalent to $44.51 an hour. Not bad for a nineteen-year-old kid with no skill set or college education. You had to be willing to travel and stay at job sites for weeks or even months, which I viewed as a positive. It helped me get out of my mom's house and away from some of my troubled friends, so I took the job.

The first thing they did was vaccinate me for every known disease since we would be working in the sewers. I remember I couldn't move my left arm for a couple of days after receiving all the shots. The next job they had was in a small Missouri town for a couple of weeks. I recall originally peering into the manholes and thinking, "this literally stinks." Well, my boss noticed my reaction and warned me that if I hesitated to jump down in the manhole, he would fire me and send me home. From that point on, I was pushing the other guys out of the way so I could be the first one down that smelly hole. We would pressure wash and clean the manholes, then conduct flow tests on the sewer lines and if there was a leak, we would send a device down to seal it. The sealing compound was called "Q-SEAL," and it was quite toxic. I don't believe it's legal to use in the U.S. anymore. If you had unprotected contact, it would affect your central nervous system. Even on hot days I always wore a full hazmat suit, gloves and a respirator when working with it. Some of the other guys didn't, a few would even make balls out of it and play with it in their bare hands which was really stupid. I guess that's why they started shaking and stuttering after working with it for a while.

Job number two was in a beautiful Wisconsin town called Portage for about six months. I thought Missouri was cold but this place was another level of cold. How cold was it? So cold that you had to plug in an engine block heater on your vehicle at night to prevent the oil from freezing. That year, it was 11 degrees below zero. The record is 37 degrees below zero not including any wind chill. Whenever you see electrical outlets to plug in your vehicle outside your hotel room, it's a red flag, it gets cold. I worked hard and played hard there, eventually bringing my motorcycle up there to ride on the warmer days.

At the end of my time in Portage, I was doing pretty well, managing to stay out of trouble and the hospital for almost a year. One Friday night I went out to a bar called "The Bar" and had a great time. At closing time, I hopped on my motorcycle in downtown Portage, where the speed limit was 25 mph. I did a burnout and sped off as fast as I could just to look cool. Well, the police officer at the end of the street didn't think it was cool and came after me with the lights flashing and siren howling. At that time, I had two choices; stop or go faster. I had installed a switch so I could turn off my tail light while still keeping the front light on just for situations just like this. Going faster seemed like a good idea at the time, so that's what I did until I noticed a few police cars blocking the road about half a mile ahead of me. Well, the cop that started chasing me was now probably a mile or more behind me so I figured I'd turn around and lose them on a back street. As I spun the bike around the left engine casing scraped the street, then I felt oil running on my shoe so it was time to stop. The cop chasing me asked why I ran. I just said that I wasn't running; I always drive this way. I don't think he bought that, but it didn't matter at that point. I was locked up overnight and the next morning I found myself standing in front of a judge facing a list of charges. The judge fined me $300 and instructed me to pay it within thirty days. Well, I knew I was leaving Portage the next week and never paid. Guess I need to avoid family trips to Wisconsin for the rest of my life. Lucky there wasn't a network of computers like they have today, I'd probably still be on their radar.

The next job was in Grandview, Indiana. That town recently had a new sewer system installed and was featured on the TV show *60 Minutes* because the contractor had made serious mistakes. A lot of leaks occurred and some of the pipes ran uphill. Two things all plumbers should know; payday is on Friday and sewage doesn't run uphill.

It was a small town and we stayed there for a few months to evaluate and repair the system as best we could. On Halloween 1980, I decided to visit the nearest big city, Owensboro, Kentucky and go party. I was driving a company truck from bar to bar and while taking a shortcut across a field I was stopped by the local police. At that point I landed in the Owensboro jail, which was constructed in 1886 using large blocks of stone and brick. Just a little fact about that jail, in 1936 it was the site of the last public hanging in the United States, hopefully it wasn't some Yankee cutting across a field. They were not as efficient as Wisconsin and I sat in a small cell for ten days without a shower, toothbrush or comb, still in my Halloween clothes... smelly, dirty and greasy. I was there on November 4th, my twenty-first birthday, so I had plenty of time to reflect on where my life was headed that day. I knew that when I got out of this mess, I needed to make major changes in my life. If I didn't, I felt like I was facing three paths; prison, the hospital or death. I was just so tired of trouble.

Finally, I found myself standing in front of a judge with a public defender. I had just met the defender minutes before we went into the courtroom. Also, I believe that I may have been one of his first or second cases ever. I would have done better having Forrest Gump representing me. He immediately started frustrating the judge with his confusion; he didn't know anything about my case. It was so bad that the judge stopped him mid-sentence and looked at me for a long, hard minute. Then the judge told me he wanted me out of his city, his county and his state. If he found me back here again, he said he would "throw away the key!" The public defender and me walked out of the courtroom together. When I asked him what just happened? He replied, "I don't know, but if I were you, I would get out of here." After retrieving my personal belongings from the police station across the street, I purchased a Greyhound bus ticket and began my journey back to St. Louis. I correctly assumed that I was no longer employed and they had moved on.

On my way to St. Louis, the bus had a layover in Evansville, Indiana at about 2 o'clock in the morning. I was worn out and dozed off at the bus station. After not showering for close to two weeks I smelled like an outhouse and was looking pretty ripe. I woke up to a guy striking me with a long, heavy-duty flashlight. Come to find out he was a young, overachieving cop that mistook me for a homeless guy. I think most homeless people probably looked and smelled better than me at that point. They took me to the hospital, where I had some of my head shaved and received eight stitches at no charge. Now I was really looking good. Afterward, they provided me with a free ride to the local jail, I think they call it Hoosier Hospitality. The next day was Monday, Veterans Day and the court was closed, so I sat there for another twenty-four hours. On Tuesday, I finally stood in front of a judge. He asked me whether I was guilty or not guilty. I was being charged with public intoxication, even though I hadn't had a drink for almost two weeks. I asked the judge what would happen if I pleaded not guilty. He said I would go back to jail and have to make bail. If I pleaded guilty, I would have to pay a $25 fine and could leave. I chose to pay the fine, even though it was almost all the money I had. I was released and went back to the bus station, then jumped on the first bus going to St. Louis.

One time I remember asking Darby what the worst part about being deployed in the field while in the Army and she said, "When you smell so bad because you haven't had a shower for a week and you can't get away from yourself." Well, that's exactly how I felt and then some. It's November 13th, same clothes on, no shower or toothbrush for 14 days. At least I didn't have to worry about a comb since some of my head was shaved and I had some beautiful stitches to highlight my part.

After finally arriving in downtown St. Louis, I proceeded to hitchhike back to my mom's house, which was 16 miles away. I was on Highway 70 when someone threw a bottle out of a car, hitting me hard on the leg. As you can imagine, it wasn't a good couple of weeks for me. Maybe some higher power knew that this is what it would take to make me change my path in life and getting hit by the bottle was just the exclamation point!!!!!!

Finally, had some good fortune. After getting back on the highway limping, with my thumb out I was picked up by some hippies in a panel van with Led Zeppelin playing on the radio and shag carpeting inside. They drove me right to my mom's doorstep. I told my mom that I needed to shower and sleep. I promised I would tell her everything in the morning, which I did. I knew that I had to make some serious life changes.

In May of 2024, I had an interview for my Global Entry pass. It classifies you as a "Trusted Traveler," thus avoiding waiting in line at customs and immigration when coming back into the country. The first question they ask is, "Have you ever been arrested?" Should I simply give them a copy of this book and hope they understand? I'm not overly optimistic about getting approved, but it's worth a shot. I still haven't heard back from them yet.

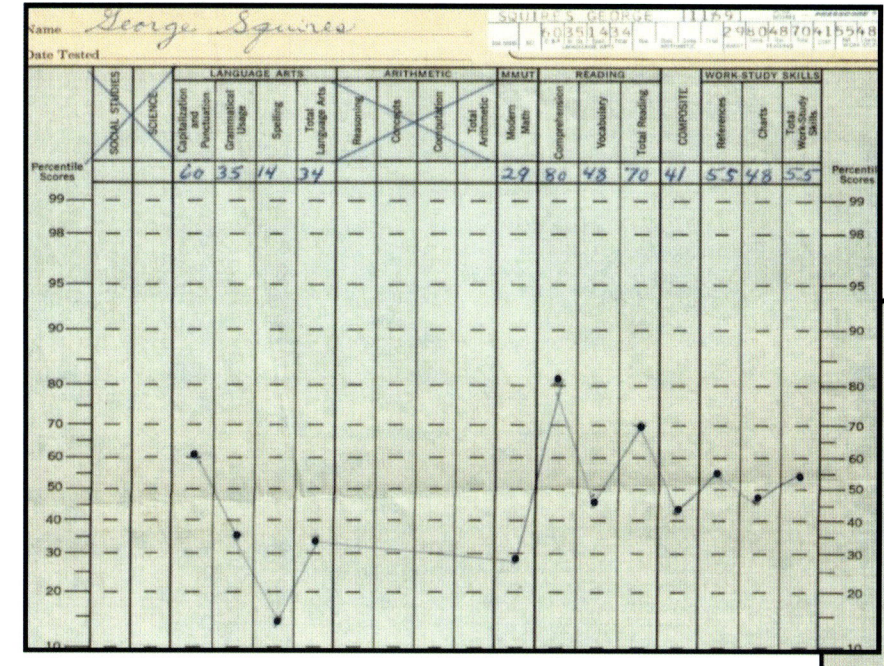

			LANGUAGE ARTS				ARITHMETIC				MMUT	READING				WORK-STUDY SKILLS		
	SOCIAL STUDIES	SCIENCE	Capitalization and Punctuation	Grammatical Usage	Spelling	Total Language Arts	Reasoning	Concepts	Computation	Total Arithmetic	Modern Math	Comprehension	Vocabulary	Total Reading	COMPOSITE	References	Charts	Total Work-Study Skills
Percentile Scores			60	35	14	34					29	80	48	70	41	55	48	55

Low on spelling but high on comperhension, my teacher at that time told me I would never make it in life unless I could spell. Well then along came spell-check, KAT is now CAT and I'm doing pretty well.

My dream machine, a red Sears Colt Mini-Bike

BERKELEY SCHOOL DISTRICT
SQUIRES, GEORGE C.
NAME
8239 CADILLAC
ADDRESS
JANUARY AT BITTEROOT
Bus Stop
George Squires
SIGNATURE

1973-74

School ID

Berkeley School District

Joe R. Cox, Superintendent

6001 Berkeley Drive
Berkeley Missouri 63134

Mr. and Mrs. Carl Squires
8239 Cadillac LA
Berkeley, MO 63134

Subject George Squires

Dear Mr. and Mrs. Squires:

George was suspended from school for five days, today for fighting.

He is to remain at home until Thursday, May 16. If you have any questions concerning this matter, feel free to contact me.

Your cooperation in this matter will be appreciated.

Cordially yours,

Gary Starr

Gary Starr
Assistant Principal
Berkeley Junior High School

It was 100% self defense

Junior High Class Picture (no it's not a mugshot)

Irene Squires High School Math Teacher in the 70's

Cat named Kitty that lived
with my mom for 20 years

Paul Squires in Grade School

Death Machine, really fast and fun Go-Cart

George Squires Classy High School picture

I'm leaving because I feel like a prisioner here & I don't like moving here and then moving again in 3 ~~month~~ months. I know if they catch me I will be in troulbe so I will try to get a job and stay out of troulbe. I will be ok.

George

George's run away note...WOW my mom and dad saved it!

This is what my dad passed out to try to find me, yes that is how I looked and the jeep behind me is what I hot wired

Undercover officer shoots, kills man after drug sale

By THOMAS D. PAGANO
Globe-Democrat Staff Writer

A 20-year-old Ferguson man was shot and killed Thursday night moments after he sold a St. Louis County undercover detective about 1,000 tablets of what was believed to be LSD, authorities said.

Curtis F. Stewart, of the 1400 block of North Elizabeth Avenue, was shot once in the chest at 6:05 p.m. when he pulled a .22-caliber pistol from a coat pocket and pointed it at undercover Detective Kenneth McPortland, 28, who had identified himself as an officer, police said.

Police gave this account:

McPORTLAND had just bought the tablets for $1,350. Moments after the transaction was completed, McPortland pulled his badge, drew his pistol and identified himself as a county police officer.

Stewart took one or two steps backward, pulled the pistol from his pocket and pointed it at McPortland. McPortland fired once, striking Stewart in the chest.

The incident occurred in the driveway of a home in the 1400 block of Charlotte Drive, a private subdivision in an older section of Ferguson. Stewart was pronounced dead at County Hospital.

STEWART WAS KNOWN to have stayed periodically at the residence and had chosen it as the location for the transaction, which was monitored by two other undercover detectives in a car about a half-block away.

"To the best of my knowledge, so far, Detective

McPortland acted in a proper manner," Detective Sgt. John McCrady said.

McPortland was selected as the 1979 Police Officer of the Year by the Missouri Peace Officers' Association last April.

Several neighbors said Stewart did not appear to be a troublemaker and that his selling drugs surprised them. One neighbor said, "He was not a kid who caused trouble in our neighborhood. As a matter of fact he was usually very friendly and willing to help out."

Ferguson police said the upper-middle-class neighborhood is normally quiet.

Curtis Stewart

Curt's last stand

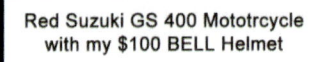

Red Suzuki GS 400 Mototrcycle
with my $100 BELL Helmet

My brother Paul Squires in
Junior High,
for some reason his
nickname was Red

George hanging out
in about 1977

4'X8' mural I hand painted that burned up in the Condo fire

Carl Squires in the 70's

52

Driver's Ed Teacher, that helped me get a HS Degree

Dick Kelle
Fran Martin
Denny Stau

Parkway
DRIVER EDUCATI
Gilbert Buick-Opel

Don Hugo
Assistant Principal
of Student Services

Mr. Hugo took an insterest in me...
sometimes that was good,
somestimes not.
Bet he would be surprised were I
ended up!

George and his new GS 750L Suzuki

Last public execution in 1936 next to Ownsboro jail,
there was over 20,000 people there, quite a show.
I bet the concsession stands made a killing!

Wisconsin
Portage

Michigan

Illinois

Indiana

Evansville

St Louis

Missouri

Owensboro

Kentucky

George's trail of trouble and path to the road of enlightenment

A journey that I never want to take again

53

Chapter 3

The 80's - Road to Enlightenment

I WAS TIRED OF CONSTANTLY BEING IN TROUBLE and getting banged up. I knew that if I kept running with my old friends and making the same kind of choices, there would just be more of the same. As I shared, I had a lot of time to do some soul searching and reflect in that 1886 Kentucky jail.

So, a couple of days after returning to St. Louis, I went down to the local military recruiting station. First, I went to the Marine recruiter's desk. They were glad to see me until I started recounting the highlights of my past few years. I assumed they would do a background check, so I wanted to be honest with them. The recruiter quickly informed me that I was not a suitable candidate. As I was leaving, the Army recruiter who was at the far side of the room said, "We accept anyone son, let's talk." However, after I shared a bit more about my history, he said that the Army wouldn't accept me either. I thought the military's job was to mold young people, guess at that point they thought I was not moldable. In hindsight it was probably not a good fit anyway.

Without a job, very little money and only a high school education, I felt my options were limited. I knew Rich, my good friend from high school was going to college at Southeast Missouri State in Cape Girardeau (SEMO). I had passed through there about a year earlier and had a fun time. Probably not how most people choose a college, but for me it was as good as any. I jumped on my motorcycle and rode down there in December of 1980, braving the freezing cold, during a huge snowstorm. It was snowing so hard that cars were pulling off the highway. Halfway down, I had to pull into a little roadside coffee shop to thaw. The waitress helped me remove my gloves and helmet, I was frozen but was determined to reach my destination that day. Later that week I enrolled in the spring semester at SEMO, which changed my life. It provided me with a new focus, new friends and a positive direction.

New Digs, New Friends, New Direction

Rich and I found a small, moldy, subterranean apartment for $125 a month ($62.50 each). I splurged on a space heater, while Rich had a couch and TV. We built a coffee table using some old 2"x 4" lumber that I had scavenged, then picked up some pots and pans at a thrift store. It was too cold to continue riding the motorcycle, so I pulled it into my bedroom and took the opportunity to dismantle it down to the frame and clean it. My mom and dad agreed to pay my tuition, which was $174 for that semester and they sent me $75 each, every month for living expenses.

After paying my basic bills, I realized I had little money left for food and entertainment. Rich and I started buying noodles and cheese, but then had to at times substitute margarine for the powdered cheese to stretch our money. I knew I had to get a job and generate some additional income. After considering my options and primarily driven by hunger, I landed a job at Callahan's Reef Seafood Restaurant as a dishwasher. I received one free meal a day and earned minimum wage. It was a new restaurant in town, and the cooks were inexperienced in preparing seafood. After washing dishes, making ceviche and shucking oysters, I would offer constructive comments regarding how I thought things should be done. In just a few weeks after opening the kitchen was struggling, by that time I had the owner's attention and he promoted me to manage it. I learned to how cook at an early age to help feed my brother and myself. This was thanks to my mom, who was very intelligent and worked long days, but struggled with cooking. It was great, more money, more food and I hired friends like Rod to work with me. I ended up working in several restaurants throughout college.

While employed at a restaurant called Jonathan's I was melting a five-gallon cube of grease on the steak grill that I intended to put in the deep fryer. The grease was in a large pot that I forgot about and it overflowed into the flaming grill, creating a major grease fire. Jenny says that sometimes I leave the stove on, well this was much worse. A server came up to me in the walk-in freezer and very casually said, "by the way, your kitchen's on fire" ...oh shit. I ran up there and encountered huge flames, like the gates of hell greeting me. The automatic fire suppression system had already been activated, but it wasn't sufficient. So, I had one of my loyal, albeit not so smart, employees wrap himself from head to toe in wet tablecloths. Then I instructed everyone to gather all the fire extinguishers in the building and we attacked the fire while he removed the large pot filled with boiling, overflowing, flaming oil from the grill. Maybe this was life number 1 out of 9 for that guy. We didn't open again that week; it was a mess.

Later, I also worked at Tinley Appliances and as a tutor in the Engineering Department. No matter what job I was hired to do; sewer rat, dishwasher, refrigerator delivery guy, cook, party organizer or teacher, I always tried to do the job to the best of my ability.

Springtime in Cape

College was going well, and I had met some great people. Terry, Jim and Kip were my next-door neighbors. There were all kinds of great college activities, we were across the street was a bustling college bar called *The Sidewalk* and the weather was getting warmer. I always disliked cold weather; I would fix that later by moving to California.

I started out as an Art Major and even though I was competent, perhaps even better than many of my peers, I believed that only a very small percentage of individuals would be able to make a good living by pursuing art as a career, most would not. Cutting off an ear and living in a car was not a good career path, so I felt I needed to reconsider my major. Vincent van Gogh was a great artist but he died broke and mentally unstable. *One of the keys to finding yourself and being successful is to be willing to try things, then adjust or change especially early in life.* The major I thought I would be good at was Industrial Technology in the Engineering Department. Drafting was a way for me to build on my artistic talent. I excelled in math; my mom held a master's degree in the subject, so maybe that was in my genes. Subjects like statistics, inventory control, calculating production rates, quality control, and time and motion studies sounded challenging but interesting. Also, as I shared, I've always been interested how machines, materials, electronics and stuff works, so this was right up my ally. I would later go on to earn a double minor in Management and Marketing, which I ended up using more in life.

In May of that year I moved out of my moldy basement apartment and in next door, above ground with Terry, Kip, and Hank the dog. I was Terry's best man a few years later, despite his wife not caring much for me. I remember one day Terry came home and told me that Julie was pregnant. I jokingly remarked, "Are you happy, or do you want to push her down the stairs?" I was one hundred percent kidding. A few months later, in the heat of an argument, I found out he said, "Julie, you're lucky you are not with George; he said he would just push you down the stairs!" Terry, why did you say that? I believe that was taken out of context, but it's hard to put that genie back in the bottle. Later, I believe she shared that with her family, so their wedding reception wasn't really warm and fuzzy for me. The union didn't last. Julie remarried and Terry married Tammy a few years later. Terry and I are still great friends.

I had a few roommates cycle through, such as Jim, Rod, Lewie, Bones and Bob. I'm still friends with all of them. The house was in a great location situated next to a bar, the college dorms, fraternity houses and within walking distance to all the classes, so it easy to find quality roommates. I started riding my motorcycle again that spring and met Jeff, who has been my best man twice now. I'm not expecting a third time. We would ride our motorcycles down county roads like the Trail of Tears and on Friday afternoons we would attend college beer busts. If you had a full tank of gas and a few dollars in your pocket, you were set. It was a fun, simple time.

We had an interesting collection of pets in Cape. Lucy, a Red-Tailed Boa snake that was about eight or nine feet long, large two iguanas Simon and Garfunkel, a large tarantula (he wasn't one of my favorites since when you took him out, he would shoot hair out, it's called urticating and would make you itch). Along with three fish tanks with African Cichlids and Hank the dog, who was hit by a mail truck when he was a puppy and thus hated anyone in a uniform including Mormon missionaries in white shirts…which wasn't always a bad thing.

The snake and iguanas where in large 6'X 2' retail glass show cases that every now and then would need to be cleaned. One day while cleaning Lucy's cage I put her in a tree in the front yard. I was cleaning the cage and then cleaning the house, just listening to the local Rock'n'Roll station when a newsflash interrupted the music; "There has been a giant snake sighted on Sprigg Street, traffic is stopped and you should account for small pets and children." Well what a coincidence I live on Sprigg Street and I have a snake, better go check on Lucy. She had disappeared, about that time a couple women came running down the street looking for their kids. Keep in mind Lucy was a little over eight feet long, big but not like the movie *Anaconda*, kids were not on the menu, but I would be worried about your kitty cat. I started looking and there were a couple guys across the street that thought finding a big snake would be cool, they found her in a creek about 150 feet from the house so problem solved…right?

I took her inside and placed her back in the case, when I came out there was several police cars on the street in front of my house and policemen walking around the area. I quickly explained Lucy was my pet and showed them the zoo we had in the house. They seemed satisfied that the monster was in a cage, but before they left they found marijuana plants on my next-door neighbor's screened in porch. They were Rod's plants but Rich also lived there. As they were carrying them out Rich walked up, I believe he was whistling and smiling on this nice sunny Missouri day…until one of the cops asked if he lived there and what about the plants. Well he freaked, "they're not mine, I don't know anything about them, I'm going to graduate." I think the cops though it was funny and just said whoever owns these plants can come down to the station and pick them up. As they were loading the plants in the police car another guy pulled up and told the cops that the snake was his and it was a fourteen-foot python. He became very insistent that I had his snake so at that point we all paraded into my living room and I showed him Lucy, a boa not a python. The police looked at him and asked the obvious question…did you lose a giant python? Which he hesitantly replied "yes, just a few months ago." The police took he down to the station and I never heard from the guy or police again. The local newspaper did call me and we did an interview, shortly thereafter the city council tried to ban exotic pets but it never did pass.

So, for those people that wondered what happened to Lucy here's the skinny. The snake was getting just too big, so I decided to sell her and took her to the pet store that Terry worked at. By the way, Lucy was always well fed and was growing fast since Terry was my free rat connection. When I brought Lucy to the store, I was handling her, she was very tame, my brother Paul had her since she was the size of a pencil. I'd take her to parties and she was the most social snake there ever was. As I had her out a guy came up and wanted to hold her so I let him. After a few minutes and girl came over and told the guy, his name was Mike, to put the snake down "we are looking at puppies, so put it down and I mean now! Do you understand, I said now!" He told her that he was just looking and gave Lucy back.

It just so happened I was there a couple days later when Mike came back in and bought the snake. I had priced it at $300, a lot of money back then, I figured that I'd maybe get half that. But Mike paid full price, he didn't even want to negotiate. He said all he heard from his fiancé for the last two days is how dare he even touch that snake. I saw him about a month later and asked him how Lucy was, he said she was great. Then I asked him how his fiancé was? He said "she's gone, that was the best $300 I ever spent!"

As you can probably tell by now, I'm not a good rule follower. I do take rules, laws and directions as rough guidelines…but who made them and why didn't I get a vote? Case in point; I've always been a pretty healthy guy, but when I was twenty-three years old down in Cape Girardeau, I had terrible allergies so I opted for surgery that basically scraped my septum/cartilage which is the inside of your nose. It's called Septoplasty. At that time, it was an operation that they kept you in the hospital overnight, unlike today where most operations short of open-heart surgery are out-patient. They were concerned about bleeding and wanted to monitor me. Coming out of the operation with my nose stuffed with gauze they rolled me into a room with another guy that just had colon surgery, probably had his rectum dissected or something similar since his bodily waste was going into a jar next to his bed. I believed the hospital paired us up since I couldn't smell and he was comatose. As they bought in dinner, I notice all I had was green Jell-O…hey I didn't have colon, bowel, stomach, throat or any other operation of that type so I asked for something else. Twenty-four hours before surgery you're not allowed to eat so I was really hungry and Jell-O just didn't cut it. The nurses said that's what the doctor ordered, so it is what it is! That didn't go over well with me, so time to find a solution. After the nurse left, I slipped on my clothes, went down to the parking lot and jumped in my 1972 green Ford F150 truck, with my nose packed with cotton gauze and a large band aid over part of my face. Then I headed for a McDonald's drive through. After devouring a Big Mac, fries and a milkshake I made my way back to the hospital room. I slipped in like a navy seal going into an enemy camp. They came in a few minutes later and asked where I had been? I told them just walking around the hospital, but they could probably still smell the

Big Mac on my breath and weren't happy. After that I was heavily monitored and feed Jell-O until I checked out the next evening. So much for stupid rules.

I joined the Sigma Tau Gamma fraternity. I never imagined I would join a fraternity, but the Sigma Tau's were good guys. I still keep in touch with many of them today. I was the Social Chairman one year, we raised money by organizing beer busts, mud wrestling, food drives, along with many other events. The local beverage distributor wanted to attend our chapter meeting one day, where they awarded us a plaque for purchasing 313 kegs in less than ninety days. Those guys were quite proud of that, just shows where a college kid's priorities lie. I believe that involvement in fraternity activities, along with various jobs and maybe even some of my past illegal endeavors were crucial in developing my organizational and delegation skills. In 1985, I was voted "Active of the Year," which was the fraternity's highest honor.

Interesting Events

The fraternity had annual float trips down the Current and White rivers. There's nothing better than enjoying a clear, hot spring day in a canoe on those pristine Missouri backwoods rivers. One year, I showed up to the float with half of my beard shaved off, right down the middle. I don't know what kind of statement I was making, but it looked cool. In hindsight, I wouldn't recommend it. Half of my face was sunburned and the other half was bright white the next time I shaved. Guess I've made worse decisions.

Every year the Sig Tau's had an annual Pig Roast at Appleton Creek. One year, we were having the Roast and Jeff brought his large tent for us to stay in. Everyone was setting up next to the creek, Jeff mentioned that it wasn't advisable to set up a tent on low ground. Therefore, we opted for a hill overlooking the campground. It was raining hard all night and the next morning there was a flash flood. If you haven't seen one it's amazing, happens in a "flash" and I had a great view from the top of the hill. The water rose about ten feet over the banks in minutes. All the other tents, food and coolers below us were washed away. I barely managed to get the beer truck out of there. Keith, whose nickname is Hobbit, was lucky enough to hook-up with a girl and return to town the prior night. But Hobbit wasn't always known for his luck. He had left his new, recently inherited car at the Roast and now it was underwater. I picked him up and took him back there, by that time the water had receded enough that you could see the top of the car's roof. We came back the next day and towed it back to town. He told me he was going to fix it, but there was no way that was happening. The next day, someone spray painted "S.S. Minnow" on it. He was flaming mad; adding insult to injury, the car never drove again. That was the way a Hobbit's luck ran back then. We still keep in touch and he's doing well. I believe his luck has turned around; he's happily married, has a new house and is growing legal marijuana in Missouri.

I also participated in the Southeast Missouri Fight Night. It was a mix of competitors, some guys who had never boxed before and some were already Golden Glove champions. In my first year, I lost my initial match. Ouch! I made it to the semi-finals in the second year. My third year I was on a mission, dedicating myself to intense workouts and training. I could run a sub-five-minute mile, lifted weights, worked on a body and speed bag almost every day. I was trained by a Bill, a Golden Gloves champion, which also made a big difference. He would teach me about timing, how to be aware of how people breath, multi-directional movement, punching in combination and never stop hitting until your competitor is on the mat. It's called the sweet science. In the following two years, I won the Super Welterweight 147-154 class without anyone going the distance; all victories were by Knockouts or TKOs.

There are a lot of great stories, but there is one more that I want to share. Rod, Lewie and I were at Twin Trees Park, just having a good time on a Friday afternoon. Out of the blue a guy on a riding lawn mower, wearing a John Deere baseball cap, approached Rod's new S10 Chevy truck, wrote down the license plate number and then drove off. Well, Rod wasn't happy about that and we became concerned. About that time, the sky started to turn dark. We jumped into the truck, but instead of heading back to town Rod decided to follow the guy on the lawnmower. He caught up to him, passed him, then Rod slammed on his brakes. I was looking out the back window and had a front-row seat as the guy's eyes bugged out with fear. He hit the truck and after face-planting on the top of the mower, then he popped back up like a jack-in-the-box and bounced off. After which he passed us on the left side and disappeared into the now pouring rain. We were stopped and all of a sudden it turned pitch black, the rain was coming down in buckets, it sounded like a train was coming at us. The truck started to shake and lift. After a few minutes the rain stopped and it became light again.

In the field next to us, about 50 to 100 yards away, there was a golf course that showed signs of a tornado ripping through it. Huge hundred-year-old trees snapped in half and grass torn up in circles. Across the river we could see that it had sliced through more trees, cutting a path that lined up with where we had originally been parked. It felt like a scene from *The Twilight Zone.*

But that's not the end of the story. A couple of miles down the road, we caught up with the John Deere hat guy on his riding mower again. He pulled into a lot next to the Mississippi River that had a single-wide trailer and jumped off the mower. It glided into the lot unmanned, as if it had a mind of its own. He ran into the trailer with a pig tied to the front porch and hundreds of five-gallon plastic buckets in the yard. Rod wanted to go in, but Lewie and I said we didn't think it was a good idea so we weren't going with him…but he went to the door anyway. As the door opened, he slipped in, about ten minutes later he came out and said, "you've got to see this." Lewie still wouldn't go in, but my curiosity got the best of me. Inside of the trailer there were what appeared to be pork and chicken bones picked clean and scattered over the floor along with large piles on the countertop. There were family pictures on the walls and tables, some probably twenty years old, all with our riding lawnmower guy wearing his John Deere hat. Come to find out, the guy lived with his mom and dad, maybe originally brother and sister. Keep in mind that we were in the backwoods of Missouri. We had gone from *The Twilight Zone* to *The Hills have Eyes!*

We learned that the son collected license plate numbers; he had thousands written down. They showed us the list and were very proud of it. Of course, the dad had to have a hobby as well; he collected five-gallon buckets. I collect magnets from all over the world, so who am I to judge other people's hobbies. You just can't make this stuff up.

Rod wanted to take the pig as payment for the damage to his truck, but that idea was a non-starter for them. I asked Rod, "what would you do with a pig?" he said to take it to a butcher. The pig wasn't looking very healthy, you could see its ribs, I believe it would have cost more money to fatten it up than it was worth. I convinced Rod that purchasing bacon at the grocery store would be more convenient and potentially more cost effective. Moving out of the path of that tornado was pure luck, number 6 of my 9 lives, if my math is correct.

After Graduation in Cape

After graduating with a 3.42 GPA in 1985, I didn't know what I wanted to do. I was dating a girl named Karmen for the last three years. She wanted to return to St. Louis, a common choice for many SEMO graduates, but I didn't share the same desire. One day she gave me a choice, St. Louis and marriage or the road. I have a theory; guys settle down based on timing as much as who they are with and it just wasn't my time.

Now I had stayed out of trouble for years, but that was about to change. One night while heading back from the Purple Crackle Bar across the river in Illinois I was pulled over for drinking and driving. I almost forgot what a holding cell looked like. This one was the same as others; no window, no room service and forget about the mint on the pillow. I was essentially compelled to stick around to resolve that issue when I came across an opportunity to invest the money that I had received from my parents for graduation in a new restaurant with an older gentleman named Kipp. I put the place together from scratch. Everything from buying the equipment, organizing the bar, creating the menu and naming it; The Earthquake Pub. Why Earthquake Pub? Well, for those who may not know Missouri history:

The New Madrid earthquakes were the biggest earthquakes in American history. They occurred in the central Mississippi Valley by Cape Girardeau, Missouri but were felt as far away as New York City, Boston, Montreal, and Washington D.C. President James Madison and his wife Dolly felt them in the White House. Church bells rang in Boston.

In the known history of the world, no other earthquakes have lasted so long or produced so much evidence of damage as the New Madrid earthquakes. Three of the earthquakes are on the list of America's top earthquakes: the first one on December 16, 1811, a magnitude of 8.1 on the Richter scale; the second on January 23, 1812, at 7.8; and the third on February 7, 1812, at as much as 8.8 magnitude.

After the February 7 earthquake, boatmen reported that the Mississippi actually ran backwards for several hours. The force of the land upheaval 15 miles south of New Madrid created Reelfoot Lake, drowned the inhabitants of an Indian village; turned the river against itself to flow backwards; devastated thousands of acres of virgin forest; and created two temporary waterfalls in the Mississippi.

Our earthquakes in California are nothing compared to what happened in the Midwest at that time.

The Earthquake Pub was located across from the college dorms and was an instant success. Location, location, location. We didn't have a hard liquor license, so I put six exotic beers on tap along with a few standards like Bud, Miller, and Pabst. We always had a great playlist going. Think of a mini Yardhouse restaurant model long before anyone else was doing that. I would use word of mouth, nightly specials, signs around campus and fliers to market it. Once on St. Patrick's Day, I bought 10 gallons of green paint and went out to the busy street in front of the Pub at 3am, painting it green from curb to curb. The police showed up that morning and asked if I did that? Did what? Oh, the street, well sure I did. For some reason, they didn't like my creativity. The next night I did my best to wash the green off the street, but it lingered around for another few weeks or more. Yes, we were packed that St. Patrick's Day!

I remember the day I popped out of the kitchen at the Pub, January 28, 1986 just before lunch and was watching the TV mounted behind the bar, all of a sudden…WOW, the space shuttle Challenger broke apart and disintegrated. We decided not to open up that day, everyone was shocked. One of those moments you will always remember.

The Earthquake Pub was busy and making money, the problem was I didn't want to live in the cold Midwest. That next summer with my savings and after cashing out my stake in the Pub I had enough money to travel. California, here I come.

Going to California

Led Zeppelin fourth album, side two, third song:

Made up my mind to make a new start
Going to California with an aching in my heart
Someone told me there's a girl out there
With love in her eyes and flowers in her hair

After deciding to head west, it was time to tackle the logistics. I had my GS750L Suzuki motorcycle and some cash. Rod was already living in San Bernardino, California and he said that I was welcome to stay at his new condo with beautiful mountain views. So, I organized a plan to travel across the country with Mike, a college acquaintance; his nickname was Hooter. His dream was to become a major star in Hollywood. Brad Pitt is from Missouri, so why not Mike? I bought a small trailer from Terry and hooked it to Hooter's Ford Escort in the summer of 1986. After traveling less than 50 miles, we quickly realized that his car couldn't tow the motorcycle and all our belongings. So, we unloaded the motorcycle and we rode it the rest of the 1,810 miles to California.

We weren't in a hurry, so we made several stops along the way. During one of our stops at the Grand Canyon, we ended up hiking from the top to the bottom and back in just one day with some German girls. It was quite a feat. These girls had been traveling the world, hiking major mountains and valleys. Luckily, we were in great shape because there's no way I could do that now. After talking with a park ranger and sharing what we had done he suggested that I apply to become a ranger also. It was an interesting idea, but California won out. Lucky for Allie, Nick, Samantha, and Darby because if I had stayed, they wouldn't exist today.

I remember stopping at the "Welcome to California" sign to take a picture. A minute later, a highway patrol officer pulled up and asked how I was doing? Then gave me a ticket for not having mirrors on my motorcycle. So, it took me less than ten minutes in California to find trouble.

Brown Air and Easy Rider

We dropped down through the Cajon Pass, similar to the Joad's in *The Grapes of Wrath* by Steinbeck. There it was, Los Angeles or so I thought. In reality, it was still 62 miles away. The smog was really bad; much worse than it is today and all I could see was brown. Hooter continued west and I headed to the address Rod had given me.

Rod said he had a beautiful home on the foothills, so when I pulled up to a trailer park, I thought I was in the wrong place. I went to the address that he had provided and a young girl answered the door. Later, come to find out she was Rod's sister, Deanna. When I asked for Rod, she said he wasn't home and wouldn't be back for a few hours. I wasn't expecting a welcoming party with balloons and a clown but I think she was surprised and didn't seem really happy to see me. After Rod returned to the trailer that night, he explained that his condo was almost completed, so we hopped into his truck, the same one that had survived the Twilight Zone tornado in Missouri and headed to his new place. As we arrived, I saw that there was just a concrete foundation and some framing in place. I guess I should have asked more questions before leaving my comfortable bed in Missouri. His place wouldn't be ready for at least a few of months. Come to find out Rod, his wife Robin, brother David, sister Deanna, and his mom and dad were all living in the trailer. So, accommodating me in this mobile estate was currently an issue. I guess it's time to hit the road and see California which turned out to be a great thing.

One thing you need to know about Rod is that he is a great promoter, salesman and optimist. I believe Jeff would agree that even if Rod's car was on fire, an earthquake destroyed his house, his dog ran away with the mailman and you asked him how his day was going, he would still say "fantastic!"

I jumped on my motorcycle and headed up the Pacific Coast Highway (PCH 1). Traveling along the California coast, with the ocean on one side, smell of salt water and the cool wind hitting you, what a beautiful ride. Kip, one of my old roommates was living in San Jose and I thought that paying him a visit him would buy me some time. After staying with him for about a month I jumped back on the bike and rode south. Traveling next to the Pacific Ocean again, camping on the beach, then stopping at the Big Sur River Inn, where you can sit on an Adirondack chair in a crystal-clear creek with cold water gently flowing around you, cooling your bare feet, eating and drinking. The place is still there and exactly the same, like a time capsule. Jenny and I stopped there on the way back from the Monterey Jazz Festival in 2022. I would highly recommend visiting it if you're traveling along the coast in the Big Sur area.

When I arrived back in Southern California Rod's place still wasn't done. His mom and dad, who took a liking to me, let me stay for a little while. After that I spent a few weeks in San Diego, Tijuana and along the coast. Growing up in Missouri, I didn't know what to expect from Tijuana. It felt like a blend of Mad Max and a disorganized swap meet. Fun but risky, so I didn't stay long. I stayed in some inexpensive hotels in San Diego and on the beach. I was becoming concerned that my money would run out so staying at the Ritz was not on my list. Finally, the condo was ready to move into. As he had advertised, it was a beautiful place in North San Bernardino with mountain views.

I Got to Get a Job

My first job in California was at the Deutsch Company in Banning as their Quality Control Supervisor. They made high-end electrical connectors; the kind used on 747 and F18 Jets. I was utilizing my degree but didn't particularly enjoy the job. It was a means to earning a paycheck, which I needed at the time. On day eighty-nine of my ninety-day probationary period my boss, George called me into his office. Wow, I thought I was getting a promotion, that was quick! Well that wasn't the case. He sat me down and said, "I'm going to do you a favor and let you go." That didn't sound like a favor, but in hindsight it was. I wasn't a good fit and the reality was that I would've never been happy there. Years later, I was able to reflect more deeply on what he did and why. Throughout your life you spend a significant amount of time at work. If you're happy, you will perform better and also lead a happier life. Sometimes people just aren't the right fit. This really hit home when I became a manager years later. If I saw George today, I would shake his hand and buy him dinner.

The next job was at Ameron Steel in their wire division as Production Control Supervisor. What I said before about working a job you don't like or that wasn't a good fit hadn't sunk in yet. I didn't like the dirty and dangerous factory, nor did I get along with most of the guys I worked with, especially my boss, Gary. But I had an important title and was making $2,000 a month, which was good money back then. By the way, having a big title is overrated.

When I was there, one person died and another one was maimed. A guy repairing the skylights fell thirty feet through the roof next to an acid bath because the fumes had corroded the metal roof above. Of course, large jacuzzi of sulfuric acid may have broken his fall if he landed in that, but the aftermath would have been really messy. Then, one morning as I turned the corner when saw a guy flopping on the ground in shock, resembling a fish out of water. I ran to him and instantly noticed blood and that he was missing fingers on one hand. Then, I looked up and saw his glove caught in a wire-pulling machine. The factory made/pulled wire; wire is made by taking a coil of steel "rod" and pulling it through a series of holes in dies that would compress it making into smaller and stronger wire. As the wire is finished it's wrapped around a huge spool about six feet tall and the motors used to accomplish this are very strong. Sometimes the wire similar to coiling up a garden hose would get off track/out of alignment. When this happens, you either stop the machine, back it up and realign or push the wire into place with a stick as it's running. Never, never, never use your hand. I cut the wire, then removed his glove from the machine, used a set of needle-nose pliers to extract his fingers and then placed them in a baggy of ice. Afterward he and his fingers were taken to the hospital. I didn't need coffee to wake up that morning.

Gary was pressuring me from day one, only to discover that he wanted his son to get the job instead of me. But I ended up getting it because I had a college degree. He did everything possible to get me to quit. Such as telling me that I had to be at work by 5:30am, even though no other manager did. Then, he assigned me an office with two small windows near the top of the ceiling, so it felt like being in a cave all day. Finally, he would change the production schedule that I had created resulting in missed delivery dates just to upset the salespeople and customers. After about a year Tamco, a Chinese company acquired the operation and I was let go. Before I left, I had documented all of his sabotage and gladly provided a detailed, well-organized copy to upper management. Shortly thereafter, I understand that he was fired and justice prevailed, even though it didn't help me. As I was driving off the property, the song *Touch of Gray* by the Grateful Dead came on the radio. It's a 1987 song about resilience in the face of challenging circumstances. The lyrics go:

Dawn is breaking everywhere

Light a candle, curse the glare

Draw the curtains, I don't care

'Cause it's alright

I will get by

I will get by

I will get by

I will survive

Every time I hear the song on my playlist, I think about Ameron. In hindsight, getting fired was a blessing.

By that time, I had moved out of Rod and Robin's condo and into a small upstairs apartment in downtown San Bernardino on 10th and D Street. It was $275 per month and included security bars on almost every window and the door. To call this a bad neighborhood would have been a compliment. The first week I was there I didn't have a landline phone yet so I went down to the corner payphone and called my dad. While

I was on the phone a guy walked up and started urinating about one foot away from me, splashing my shoes. Well I was going to get off the phone and demonstrate my displeasure but as I hung up, he just looked at me, started crying and sat in his puddle. At that point I figured he had bigger problems than me and I just walked away. Not Newport Beach by any stretch. One day I walked down to a local bar about a block away to play pool when a charming Hispanic girl approached me, asked my name and then remarked, "You are very brave." Well, if I had a dollar for every time that I've heard that in my life...well, I'd have a dollar. So, I asked her why and she said, "You're the only white guy around here." Yep, time to leave.

Another time while at Johnny's nightclub in San Bernardino, I got into a skirmish and ended up tumbling over a table, which resulted in breaking my head open. By the way it wasn't my fault, some guy sucker punched me because he thought I was someone else...sometimes saying sorry just isn't good enough and I went after him. I went to St. Bernardine's Emergency Room in downtown San Bernardino around midnight on a Saturday. It was packed with gunshot wounds, car accidents and all kinds of violent injuries. As I mentioned before, it was a rough area. I didn't want to wait until morning so I went home. After cleaning the gash above my eyebrow and realizing its depth, down to my skull, I retrieved my reliable sewing kit. Despite the intense pain, I skillfully sewed three stitches to close the wound that would have made a second-year medical student proud. Just an interesting fun fact about downtown San Bernardino, it has one of the highest crime rates in American, one's chance of becoming a victim of either violent or property crime is 1 in 23.

I had earned enough money to buy a new 1987 gray Camaro, which was a really cool car. Rod was using my motorcycle, which had over 150,000 miles on it by now and it was on the brink of death. The GS750L Suzuki had given me ten good years and many miles, taking me across the country through rain, shine and snow. Goodbye, old friend. The Camaro was a fast car and as Jeff, among a few other friends, will tell you, I'm not easy on my machines. One day I was speeding down a narrow back road in Etiwanda at over 100 mph, it was lined with towering Eucalyptus trees on both sides and I hit a five-foot railroad track berm and launched, catching some serious air. The car felt like it was up for a long minute, something out of the *Dukes of Hazzard*. When I touched down it hit hard, all frame and substructure. I slid down the road for several hundred feet, zipping along at high speed completely out of control and then landed in a ditch just inches away from the towering, immovable, huge trees. It took me a few minutes to regain my composure and to my surprise I was able to start the car. Now let's see if this thing will roll. I kept that car for another four years, after that it had a lot of problems...but still it looked great, at least on top. The next time I went to change the oil they couldn't even get the oil plug out and had to replace the oil pan along with some of the crossmembers. That should be covered under warranty, right? Life number 7 of my 9 lives.

So, No Job, Time to Have a Beer

One day I stopped into El Torito on Hospitality Lane for a beer, that's when I met John. He said he worked as a headhunter, assisting companies in finding employees. Of course, I shared with him that I was looking for a job and that I had a college degree, then I proceeded to share some details about my last two jobs, that I hated. At that point, he told me that I shouldn't work a job that I don't like because life is too short. He thought I would be good in sales and mentioned that he knew of a growing company that was looking for salespeople to market a new product, the FAX machine. It sounded interesting. I met Rod the next day and told him about the opportunity. I regarded Rod as a great salesperson, so I wanted his opinion. He thought I would do well. I remember his words, "Sales will take you to the mountaintop some days and into the deep, dark valley the next, so be prepared."

I agreed to go on the interview at Burtronics Business Systems; John and Rod helped me prepare for it. First, I showed Rod my resume that I had invested a lot of time and money in, I was very proud of it. Immediately, he threw it into the trash. He said, "this has nothing to do with the job you're applying for." Sales rule #1: If it doesn't help, don't say it, show it or do it. Then he said, "they are going to ask you why you think you would be successful." My response was, "I'm a fast learner and hard worker." His response was "no, no, no." Sales rule #2: Answer with a question if you want to control the meeting; questions control the conversation. Then he said "after a brief pause to reflect and appear to give the question deep thought, then you should say; if I worked 5 or 6 days a week, 50 to 60 hours a week, do you think I'd be successful?" After which shut up and remain silent. Sales rule #3: Whoever speaks first, loses. It went just like we had role-played it. After a long minute of uncomfortable silence, Tom, the manager interviewing me, said, "yes, I think you would be successful." Naturally, my response was, "what day do I start?" *Chance favors a prepared mind.*

When I saw John later that day, he shared that they really liked me but didn't like my beard. Well, I was much more attached to eating than to my beard, so it came off that night. I started my career at Burtronics on November 1, 1988. It was a great feeling; now I had springs in my bed every day instead of magnets. I fell in love with sales, became Salesman of the Year a couple of times and helped grow Burtronics from a million to a fifteen-million-dollar-a-year business.

Learning and Growing, Life is Good

Life was good; a lot of positive things were happening in my life. I placed eighteen fax machines in my second month at Burtronics, setting a sales record. I wanted to excel and master my new profession, so I would purchase books like *Art of the Deal* by Trump, which turned out to be a surprisingly good read. Also, I attended sales seminars conducted by Zig Ziglar, Brian Tracy and one of my favorites, Tommy Hopkins. If you want a great sales book, pick up Tommy's *Master the Art of Selling*. He once told me at a seminar; "In this profession, no one limits your income but you. Selling is the art of asking the right questions to obtain the minor yeses that enable you to guide your prospect towards the major decision. It's a simple function, and the final sale is nothing more than the sum total of all your yeses." I was motivated.

FAX sales gave me a lot of practice to hone my skills. Since it was a lower-priced item compared to higher-priced copiers, you had to make more sales to earn the same amount of income. I would meticulously map out my territory to maximize efficiency, make 30-50 cold calls daily to secure 2-3 appointments, and make 4-7 placements each week.

I went to a different laundromat every weekend to wash my clothes. After putting my laundry in the washer/dryer instead of just sitting around I would walk the local area and discreetly slip flyers advertising FAX machines under the doors of businesses. At that time there were no desktop computers so I had to handcraft the marketing flyers by cutting and pasting letters from newspapers and magazines. They looked very rough, kind of like ransom notes, but got the message across. Come Monday I would receive calls from businesses that were interested in this new thing called a FAX; no one else did that.

Another strategy I used was calling on construction contractors before 7am, prior to the secretary/gatekeeper arriving at work for the day. I knew I was in luck when the only vehicle in the parking lot was a big pickup truck and the back door was unlocked. After walking in and some guy asking or sometimes yelling at me, "who the hell are you and why are you here so early?" I would say you must be the owner and the hardest working guy here since you're already getting ready for the day. By 8 o'clock, more than once, I would walk out with an order in my hand.

When I lost a deal, I would go back to the office or get together with Rod and role-play what happened, so the next time I could be better prepared. I think between role-playing and playing Stratego, I met with Rod five or six times a week. You should never get stumped by the same situation or question the second time if you're on your game. Even a horse doesn't step in the same hole twice. One theory on why the Beatles were so good: practice, practice, practice. They would play 2 or 3 gigs a day, seven days a week, in their early years. Sales Rule #4: Do the numbers, and the results will follow.

The most important thing in sales and life is having a positive attitude. It's the lens you view the world through and the key to success. Also, my friend Enrique said that if you have a positive attitude and aura, people treat you differently. I guess it helped us get through a lot of Mexican checkpoints, so I believe it. One day, I stumbled upon a saying that I would read every morning before going to work. Here it is...what a wonderful way to begin the day!

Promise Yourself

*To be so strong that nothing
can disturb your peace of mind.
To talk health, happiness, and prosperity
to every person you meet.*

*To make all your friends feel
that there is something special in them
To look at the sunny side of everything
and make your optimism come true.*

*To think only the best, to work only for the best,
and to expect only the best.
To be just as enthusiastic about the success of others
as you are about your own.*

*To forget the mistakes of the past
and press on to the greater achievements of the future.
To wear a cheerful countenance at all times
and give every living creature you meet a smile.*

*To give so much time to the improvement of yourself
that you have no time to criticize others.
To be too large for worry, too noble for anger, too strong for fear,
and too happy to permit the presence of trouble.*

To think well of yourself and to proclaim this fact to the world, not in loud words but great deeds.

To live in faith that the whole world is on your side

so long as you are true to the best that is in you."

— Christian D. Larson

Words to live by. I still have this saying hanging in the hallway of our house today.

Out of that Dicey Hood

While still living on 10th and D Street in downtown San Bernardino one day I came home to find that most of my personal belongings were gone. If you remember, I mentioned that there were security bars on the door and the windows...except one, the bathroom. It was 18" x 24" window on the second floor, a small kid probably slipped in and grabbed everything that would fit through it. My furniture and stereo speakers were too big to take, but my shoes, shirts, toothpaste, belts, pans, receiver and lamps were all gone. When I informed my landlord that I was going to move, he said that he would install bars on the bathroom window, reduce the rent and suggested I start carrying a gun like he did. I wouldn't have stayed there if it was free, I wasn't going to miss those neighbors smoking crack or the nightly sirens and gunshots.

I moved into some new apartments near Rod and Robin's condominium, which was in a much better area. About that time, Rod and Robin decided to relocate back to St. Louis to be closer to her family. Just a side note, do you remember Hooter, the guy I came to California with? He did make it to Hollywood and was waiting tables at the Dome Club in Hollywood. I saw him twice, once in West Hollywood and again in Laguna Beach. I thought, "wow, this is nice. I'd like to live by the beach someday." I haven't seen Hooter on the big screen, so I assume he never became a movie star.

Having a sip of beer at Pig Roast, Appleton Creek, MO

GS 750L with Lucy on back

Lucy the Boa and Simon the Iguana

Hand me a beer Brother

Terry & George Sig Tau Float Trip on the Current River 1984

Rich, Bob, George and Terry Alumni Float Trip 2013

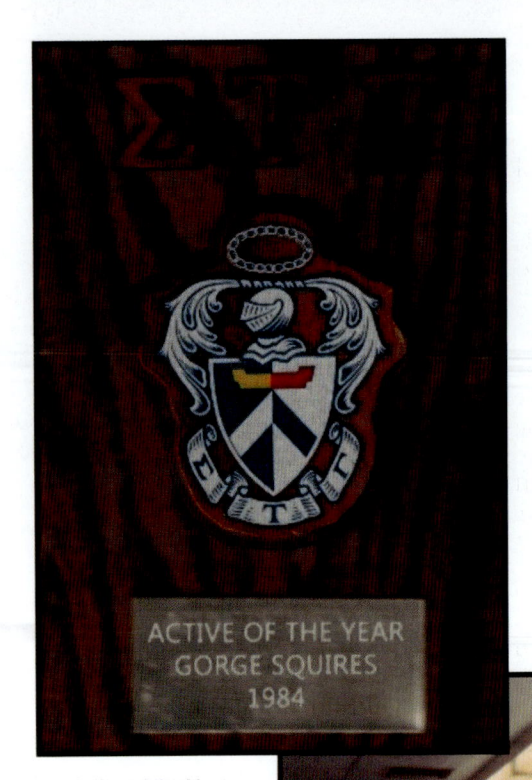

Active of the Year
Award

Sig Tau Gamma Composite
with all the Members

George & Rich
looking good

Mike (AKA Flippy) from New Zealand, he worked for me
at the Earthquake Pub. He ate 24 boiled eggs in 4 minutes
on a bet, I was laughing so hard I was crying.
Great Guy, I ended up buying him a plane ticket
back to New Zealand before I left for California.

By the way the street in back of him I painted green
for St. Patricks Day

Kip & Hank the Dog, very smart (I'm talking about the dog, just joking Kip)

Welterweight Champion in 2004 and 2005

Knockout!!!

Roomates and friends
Lewie, Jim and
Marshall

Jeff and George
outside the Earthquake Pub

SEMO College Graduation
with dad and mom,
bet they were glad to see that

Last day in St. Louis before going to California with friends

Jeff went into the Navy and I went to California

Mike (AKA Hooter) and George loading up to go to California

Pit stops along the way, very bad luck to remove any wood

Hiking the Grand Canyon with German Girls

Soaking up the Arizona sun

Sign on Hooter's car
"YEA CALIFORNIA
THAT'S IT
THAT'S THE TICKET"

Finally made it!

Robin, Rod and George on those California beaches

George and Rod unloading

In front of Rod and Robin's condo

Hot looking 1987 Camaro

Apartment on 10th and D
in downtown
San Bernardino,
my light bulb is still on
I'm surprised
it wasn't stolen

Sailing with
Perk

The Burtronics Crew

Promise Yourself

To be so strong that nothing can disturb your peace of mind.

To talk health, happiness, and prosperity to every person you meet.

To make all your friends feel that there is something fine in them.

To look at the sunny side of everything and make your optimism come true.

To think only of the best, to work only for the best, and to expect only the best.

To be just as enthusiastic about the success of others as you are about your own.

To forget the mistakes of the past and press on to the greater achievements of the future.

To wear a cheerful countenance at all times and give every living creature you meet a smile.

To give so much time to the improvement of yourself that you have no time to criticize others.

To be too large for worry, too noble for anger, too strong for fear, and too happy to permit the presence of trouble.

I still have the original "Promise Yourself"

Chapter 4

The 90's - Growing a Career & Family

THERE WERE A LOT OF HAPPY MEMORIES at Burtronics. After working as a FAX salesman for a year, I was promoted to Microfilm and Imaging. A more complicated and a longer sales process, but with bigger margins, higher commissions, along with top-notch training provided by the 3M company. The only downside was flying back to Minnesota in the cold winter to the 3M headquarters.

About that time, Burtronics hired a new receptionist, Cyndie. She helped me with some of my paperwork and according to the license plate frame on her little brown Toyota "I Love Julio," she had a boyfriend. I would never ask a married woman out, but she wasn't married and I had heard "no" plenty of times, so I decided to ask her out to lunch. Her initial response was, "I have a boyfriend." Then I asked, "would tomorrow work?" to which she affirmatively replied. Sales rule #5: It's not a major objection if it doesn't come up twice. Lunch was great, and we started to grow closer. One night under the cover of darkness, I went to her house; she was only twenty years old and still lived with her mom, Pat. I cut about three dozen roses from the front yard of a house down the street. I'm sure they weren't happy the next morning. Then, I removed her license plate frame, broke into her car then placed the frame and roses on her seats. I went home that night and looked forward to seeing her at work the next day. Well, that was the end of Julio and the beginning of George. No, I never bought her an "I Love George" license plate frame. We continued to date and a little while later she settled into my apartment.

Now, going back to my job, I was doing well and had a great boss, Barbara. Burtronics was a growing company and the owner, Perk was a great guy that I believe genuinely cared about his employees and people. I learned a lot from him. He would say, *"Take the money out of the decision and if it changes reconsider it,"* a life lesson I still use today. Another piece of advice was *"If you can't put it on the front page of the newspaper don't do it."*

My microfilm markets were mainly government and land title companies. One of my major prospects was First American Title. By the way, in sales a customer has three things; need, ability and desire, a suspect has only one of the three and a prospect has two of the three, so the logical way I looked at things I just had to create the desire for First American Title to do business with me. I truly believe sales is not luck or the gift of gab, it's a science. Every couple of weeks I would stop by their Riverside office to ask Gary, their Vice President, for an opportunity. Finally, several of his microfilm machines broke down and I brought over some loaner machines for him to use. This helped me get my foot in the door, which was all I needed. Soon after, he was evaluating the replacement of all his machines, it was a horse race between Canon and me. Gary made good decisions, but not quick decisions; this was a significant investment in his Riverside office. At this point I felt like I knew Gary better than the Canon sales representative. After testing and evaluating for over two months, it was Christmas Eve. I stopped in that day at noon. Most people had already left and the rest were packing up for the holidays. The Canon representative was probably at home enjoying Christmas cookies. So, it went something like this: "Hey Gary, Merry Christmas! When was the last time you saw the Canon guy? So, it's been a few weeks. Well, I think you wore him down. You understand that you'll never wear me down, and I'll always take care of you. Let's just get this decision off your to-do list before the holidays or I'll be waiting on your front step January 2nd, when you return." That day I walked into Burtronics with hardly anyone around and handed Tom, my Vice President a signed order for $280,000. Tom was surprised and he said nobody works on Christmas Eve. Well, that's what I was counting on. I hope the Canon guy had a good holiday. My commission was sufficient for a down payment on a house, so we purchased a distressed $94,000 HUD repo house in North San Bernardino with a 10% mortgage. Gary became a great friend; he was one of the most honest and sincere people I've ever met. Even after he left First American Title we would talk and have lunch regularly. Sadly, he passed away from cancer in 2022.

After moving into our dilapidated HUD house, which needed a lot of repairs to transform it into a cozy home, I asked Cyndie to marry me. She was beautiful, hardworking, had a good heart and impeccable timing. As I mentioned before, especially when it comes to men, settling down is about timing as well as finding the right person.

A few years later, my mom would meet Bob and they were married. Bob is a great guy who will always be like family to the kids and me. Best of all, he makes my mom happy. They traveled the world, bought a beautiful house on Lake St. Louis and have been there for everyone rain or shine.

Starting a Family as the Economy Tanks

We had Allie in June of 1990 and Nick in November of 1991, so the family was off and running. Cyndie and I were moving forward, fixing up our new house, buying a four-door car and changing a lot of diapers. Work was going well until the latter part of 1991 when there was a major downturn in the economy which impacted house sales, essentially shutting down my title company microfilm business. I was slowly going broke, facing increasing expenses and decreasing income.

One day, I was playing around in the Burtronics equipment demonstration area with a machine called a RISO. It was a high-speed digital duplicator, a rather unique system at that time, similar to an automated mimeograph. It printed 120 pages per minute and the operating cost was a fraction of the cost of a photocopier when doing longer print jobs. When I asked a copier salesperson why they weren't selling more of these he said it doesn't duplex, it doesn't sort and the first-print speed is slow. Burtronics had only installed four RISO machines at a school district in the past twelve months and were preparing to discontinue that product. I believed it was a great product. The salespeople knew every reason why it wouldn't work, but none knew why it would. In my assessment, they had positioned it incorrectly. So, I went into Tom's office and shared with him that I wanted to sell the RISO machine on a straight commission, based on earning 50 percent of the profit. I figured that if I couldn't generate sales any base salary similar to the current programs offered would just prolong my slow financial death. His response was that no one had ever asked him to work on a straight commission basis before, it was a significant risk. He knew that microfilm was becoming obsolete and shared that he wanted to transition me to copiers. At that point, I told him I was going to quit if he didn't move me to RISO. Little did he know that it wasn't an idle statement; I had already been offered a job at a payroll processing company earlier that week. I felt this was a great product for a struggling economy and I could make it a success. Well, he hesitantly agreed.

During the first month, I called on churches, schools and clubs with high printing volumes, which I believe to be my target markets and try to explain how the process worked. That it was different from a photocopier, but I was having no success. I felt it was like trying to explain blue to a blind guy. Ray Charles is a great pianist and singer, but don't ask him to pick out curtains to match your couch and he probably couldn't appreciate a high-speed printing system either. Maybe I had made a mistake; I was getting nowhere. While driving back to the office after a hard day I passed by a used Ford Bronco for sale. I told the seller that if he allowed me to take it to my office and if my RISO machine would fit in, I'd buy it. Sometimes, you just need to double down on an idea that you believe in. The next day, I was out with the system loaded up, cold calling on a church. The pastor said that donations were down and they didn't have any funds for new equipment. Of course, I was prepared for that and I knew that I had to show the system. So, I shared with him that I was not the best salesperson to try to explain how this system worked, especially since this was a new product for me. If they could just help me out by taking a look at the machine and providing some feedback, I would really appreciative it. He agreed and I rolled the RISO in to do a demonstration. Their current copier system was less than a third of the speed and eight times more expensive to operate based on their current job runs. Also, I apologized; the system was so simple and reliable that they may never know their service technician's name. The secretary loved the speed and user-friendliness, while the pastor liked that she was excited and happy. After crunching the numbers and considering a lease, along factoring in the reduced operational costs they were able to save money and the deal was finalized. Sales Rule #6: People buy mainly based on emotion, but often justify it with logic. I became very proficient at demonstrating the machine and working with the numbers. In many organizations it made sense to install the RISO system. By the end of the year, I had doubled my income.

To make Tom a true believer, the next year I bet him a Rolex watch that I could break a half million in sales. Surpassing what any commercial sales representative had achieved in any division at Burtronics.

One day, I called on Warren, the District Manager at Brunswick. He didn't want to see any salespeople, which is not a surprise since most people don't. I asked him for fifteen minutes of his time, not sixteen, not seventeen, not eighteen and if he agreed I shared with him I would never knock on his door again, he agreed. I rolled in the RISO, gave him my Seiko watch to time me, started the demonstration and I stayed true to my word. Exactly fifteen minutes later I asked him if he wanted me to stay or go. He said just wait a minute then picked up the phone and called his main office in Chicago "you got to see this machine, it's what we need." The outcome was that many of the Brunswick Bowling Alleys installed RISO's that year. Along with Brunswick I was placing RISO's at most major churches and a majority of the School Districts in Riverside County. I had my pitch dialed in and many new accounts were referrals from happy clients. It was a fun time.

After billing $512,000, I wanted my Rolex. The only problem was that Tom didn't tell Perk, the owner of Burtronics about our bet because he thought there was no way I was going to do it. I had Tom in a pickle, so the next day I offered him a solution. I had a mobile cell phone, it was a large NEC phone mounted inside my vehicle, flip phones or iPhones were inconceivable at that time. I believed it was one of the tools key to my success and productivity. Everyone else had pagers, so there was no company allowance for a phone since it was considered a luxury or toy. *I believe you need to invest in yourself and not wait for someone else to invest in you.* At seventy-five cents per minute you could rack up a substantial bill. I knew Tom was the one who personally approved my expense report, so my proposal was that if he agreed to pay my cell phone bill every month, I could live with my Seiko watch. I think I came out ahead. A new Rolex was about $2,000 back then, and my cell phone bill was over a couple of hundred dollars a month. He was off the hook. A win-win.

Management… Not Me

Burtronics had opened an office in Palm Desert, California a couple of years earlier and I would stop in when I was working with the Coachella Valley School Districts. After a few visits, I had a pretty good idea of why the office was struggling. While having lunch with Tom a few days later I asked how much sales were generated at that office the previous year? He said about $178,000, which was considered very low for having four salespeople. I shared with Tom that these guys stroll in at 9am, enjoy coffee and talk, then head out to the field for maybe a few hours. By two, they're at home watching Oprah. After which Tom said "well, why don't you fix it then?" I quickly responded, "not my problem. I was just giving you a heads up." After Ameron I was very happy doing what I was doing. There was no way I wanted to manage anybody but myself. Then he said, "do it and Burtronics will pay you an extra $2,000 a month, plus an override and you can keep your current responsibilities as well." That was enough to change my mind.

The next day, I was in the Palm Desert office at 8am, waiting for everyone to leisurely drift in. I let them get their coffee and chat about what happened the night before on the TV show *Survivor* and settle in. Then, I stood up and asked, "Who wants to make more money?" Naturally, they all responded with YES!!! "Well, I'm your new supervisor, and I'm here to help you do that!" They were enthusiastic until I outlined their new program, which required them to be in the office by 7am and out in the field by 8am. Due to the desert heat, we are starting early and I expect a full eight-hour workday. Well, the excitement level dropped off a cliff. One guy immediately stood up and told me he had been there for almost two years and he wasn't going to comply, using language I need not repeat. One of my conditions for taking the position was having full authority to hire and fire at my discretion. Right there and then, I terminated him. Of course, he called Tom, and Tom confirmed that it was 100% my decision. "So, get a box, gather your personal belongings and I'm giving you ten minutes to leave. If you don't, you'll be trespassing, your final paycheck will be sent by mail." I think I had everyone's attention at that point.

Within Sixty days, I had cleaned house and hired all new people. One of my trademark phrases was "*You can be lazy, you can be dumb, but don't be both.*" Unfortunately, the current Palm Desert staff were both and had bad habits to boot. The following year, that office surpassed one million dollars in sales.

Smooth, Happy Sailing then Settling into Palm Desert

I had gone from a troubled teen to a college graduate, landing a good job, and now a husband and father. Life was going great! Sometimes I felt it was hard to believe what a little luck and perseverance had bought me. Cyndie and I were doing well, we had time to go to Hawaii and visit Jeff and Nancy, kind of a delayed Honeymoon. Later I won a trip from one of our vendors for being one of the top salespeople in the country to the Caribbean and Florida Keys that was fantastic. I could never image being with anyone else but

Cyndie. Burtronics was a fun job, I was successful and happy there…it was smooth sailing with calm seas and a good wind blowing me along.

I was not only a good salesman but at times a good collections/repo guy when needed. I remember one time when a past due client didn't want to make payments. So, I went in their office at the end of the day, told another salesperson to keep the truck running and grabbed their copier, then to their surprise ran out the door with it. Another time with a large copier I went to talk the business owner, this guy was a problem from day one, the receptionist told me he wasn't there, then she asked me if I was a technician, sure I've worked on a copier before. She walked me back to the copier, at that point I borrowed the main wiring harness and put in my brief case. That may motivate him to pay. I figured if they weren't willing to pay their bills, they shouldn't be able to derive the benefits of the system. There were a few more stories but you get the picture, I took it personal when someone tried to cheat us.

I had great customers too. I remember one day, Michael, a guy that I helped start his business walked me out his front door, looked up at the beautiful sunset and said "you got to take a minute to smell the roses." Then he handed me a $5,000 check, it blew me away. My philosophy was; be honest, do a good job, take care of people and the rewards will follow. I had a lot of loyal customers that became friends and they stayed with me for years and years. *One thing in life you'll never regret is saying thank you.* I was always thankful to be given the opportunity to earn someone's business and thankful for all the people that helped me in business and personally in my life.

The drive from San Bernardino to Palm Desert is approximately 70 miles. After spending several hours, two or three days a week behind the wheel, I made the decision to relocate our family to Palm Desert. Now that we had Samantha and it didn't make sense for Cyndie to work. We moved into a new house with a large 16' x 36' pool. It's a necessity in the desert if you ever want to venture outside during the scorching 120-degree desert heat in the summer. Shortly thereafter, Cyndie became pregnant with Darby. Four kids in five years, Samantha and Darby were less than a year apart, so we were busy. I remember when I could fit all the kids in a wagon and pull them up to El Paso Street for ice cream. We made new friends, such as Rick and Emma, who I still keep in contact with. It was a happy time. I remember pulling into our driveway, the song playing on the radio was *Once in a Lifetime* by The Talking Heads. Some songs define times in your life.

And you may find yourself living in a shotgun shack
And you may find yourself in another part of the world
And you may find yourself behind the wheel of a large automobile

And you may find yourself in a beautiful house, with a beautiful wife

And you may ask yourself, "Well, how did I get here?"

So, What Could Go Wrong?

As I shared in my introduction, some memories are very painful to recall, but they significantly influenced my life and the way I think, so they need to be shared. The following year, my next-door neighbors moved out and rented their house to Scott and Shelby, a nice young couple with a three-year-old and a newborn baby. We would have BBQs and playdates with the kids. The neighbors on the other side were two guys and a girl who were partiers, smoking, drinking and later found I out they were using methamphetamines, also known as speed.

I think you've figured out by now that I'm no angel, but I had sown maybe not all, but most of my wild oats ten years prior. Having kids calms most people down quite a bit. Cyndie started experimenting with drugs to lose weight and have more energy. It was just a bad road, and I knew there were problems. I just wasn't aware of how significant they were yet. She started smoking cigarettes and I believe she began using speed/methamphetamines almost daily. Then, she was staying up late after I went to bed with our neighbor, Scott. I had to get up in the morning and work, so partying every night didn't fit into my life of building a career and raising a family.

Things began to deteriorate. I loved Cyndie with all my heart and it was hard to imagine how dysfunctional things were getting. I believe that sometimes people choose not to see the truth; it's called denial. I've always tried my best to perceive unfiltered reality, the real truth. What I was seeing and feeling was not good. I was concerned for her, our kids and myself. We had gone from the perfect white picket fence family to something I didn't recognize. She would go to the store for hours on end without explanation. She was taking an evening class at the College of the Desert and wouldn't return home until after midnight. At one point, I thought I was going crazy and Cyndie told me more than a few times that I was. I followed her one night in a minivan packed with all the kids and at that point I knew she was having an affair with Scott. After confronting her, I told her I was leaving unless she came clean and stopped the affair with Scott and the drugs. It hurt so, so bad. Words cannot describe it. My heart was broken, torn out and burned. I have never felt so much pain and I hope I never do again.

The next day, I went over to Scott's and confronted him. Of course, he continued to deny, deny, deny, so I told his wife, Shelby what was going on. She didn't believe anything; she was in denial and even became mad at me. This had to stop. I wasn't a big fan of guns at this point in my life and I'm still not, so I didn't have one. I went to the gun store the next day with the intention of purchasing a gun. I selected one and filled out the application form. Thank God there was a thirty-day waiting period; otherwise, there would have been one less guy named Scott on this planet and one more guy in prison.

One very important piece of advice that I want to share, which has saved me from making regrettable decisions more than once in life is; *Before you say, write or do something that has significant consequences, wait twenty-four hours*. I heard President Lincoln used this strategy. Evidently, Trump never has.

So, I needed a plan. Cyndie said it was over, which I believed. Shelby needed to see the light. Having them living next door was not an option, and the drugs needed to stop. I went to the local florist and requested some flowers, specifically dead ones from their trash can. After explaining my situation and paying top dollar they hesitantly agreed to deliver them. I had a letter attached that I asked Cyndie to write about all the times and places with Scott. I promised not to look at it, which I never did. I had the ugly, brown, brittle, dead flowers and the letter delivered to Shelby while Scott was at work to get my message across. I believe she received them, since the vase and flowers were in a hundred pieces on my front doorstep when I returned home that night. I had sent Cyndie and the kids to my mom's in Missouri for a few weeks to try to get the situation under control. I never told my parents about what happened; I felt it was easier that way. I did confide with my best friend, Jeff and my boss, Tom about what was going on. Tom had experienced a similar situation many years before and helped me through all of this. His words of wisdom, which I still carry with me today, were: "*Do not let the bad things that happen in your life bleed over and poison the good things in your life, you need to compartmentalize.*" Later, I would have other friends and employees to who I would pass this advice on to. Going through this experience I believe made me a better person; enabling me to better understand, have more empathy and help others in some of life's difficult situations.

I believe you should never hold a grudge or wish ill upon someone. Even though I wouldn't have given Scott a rope to get out of a hole, I'm not going to lie in wait and push him into one...well, I may give him a little bump. *Holding a grudge is like holding a piece of hot coal in your hands; the only person it hurts is you. Moving forward and being successful is always the best revenge.*

Scott and his family moved, but I still didn't want to stay in that house or area any longer. The memories were just too painful. I still loved Cyndie, but I couldn't trust her like I had before, at least not right away. Now, there was a crack in our crystal vase of trust. Even though nobody else could see it, I knew it was there. If we didn't have kids, I might have just packed up and left. Shortly thereafter, Tom promoted me from

Supervisor to Manager over the RISO, FAX, Computer, and Imaging/Microfilm Divisions. In light of this, we relocated closer to the main office in San Bernardino, to a charming little town called Yucaipa, California.

Starting Over and Moving Forward, I Think

In Yucaipa, we first rented a house and after about a year we bought the Golden Meadow home. Things were getting back on track, but truth be told I still wasn't 100% alright yet. I expected that would just take time. Cyndie was once again a loving wife and mother, so it seemed like we had a chance to repair and recover from this difficult situation. We sent Allie and Nick to public school, while Samantha and Darby attended a Yucaipa Baptist Christian Day Care to give Cyndie a break. That was the calm before the storm.

Cyndie met a girl who was a drug user and as a result she relapsed into drugs again. This time, it was worse minus the affair. I remember looking across the dinner table and thinking, "do I know this person?" She was losing weight; at one point, I believe she weighed less than 100 pounds. When my dad and Carol came to visit, she greeted them at the door and later they shared that they didn't recognize her at first. I would come home to our new house and she would have all the pictures taken down, rearranging them and painting the walls. They had just been painted a couple of months before. Big red flags were going off. It was hard for me to go to work because I just didn't know what the day would bring.

Finally, I had to take action. Of course, she considered me the crazy one while she kept insisting that she was perfectly fine. I shared with her mom, Pat and her brother, Mike what was going on and that I was going to take the kids to school/daycare, then come back to the house that morning and give her the option of going into treatment or getting tested for drugs. If she didn't agree, I would obtain a court order and take the kids away. At that point, she broke down and admitted using drugs, so I took her to the Loma Linda Substance, Recovery and Wellness Center that day.

Under Professional Care and the Bitter End

Cyndie was in bad shape. I had probably waited too long, but when you're in the eye of a storm it's hard to see the path. The following days, she began detoxing from the drugs. I was doing my best to take care of our kids and manage the financial damage that had occurred. We had over $50,000 in credit card debt, most of which I didn't know about until I started intercepting the mail after she left. Then I discovered that she had credit cards that I was unaware of and was still using them while in rehab. At that point I shared with Cyndie that I decided to file for divorce to stop the financial bleeding, but still wanted to try to salvage our marriage. I wasn't going to continue having this financial exposure if she wasn't being honest. I was also very transparent with her family and the hospital staff. In fact, after informing the hospital staff about my decision a couple of them asked, "If she had cancer, would you still file for divorce?" since they looked at drug use as a disease. I thought that was one of the stupidest things I've ever heard and it showed total disregard for me and especially our kids. "Yes, I would still do it if she had cancer. However, people with cancer typically don't behave this way." I was concerned that we would lose everything if I didn't take some kind of action. If you sit in these AA or rehab groups, you will hear stories about successful people and their families ending up on the street, so I believed that could happen.

The breaking point came a couple of weeks later when I asked her if she was romantically involved with any of the guys in rehab and she admitted that she was. My heart was already torn out in Palm Desert. This was bad, but I had already been numbed and it was time to move on. The divorce proceeded. My plan was to ensure that Cyndie wasn't on the street so I rented an apartment for her and her new boyfriend, Dan. She worked with me and I assumed all the debt, also I was able to keep the kids in the house and have custody. We didn't have much money at that point but I did my best to make sure she was financially ok until she could find a job. It was a tough time.

Dan turned out to be a good guy. Cyndie and Dan ended up getting married, but years later they were divorced. He passed away young; I believe due to his previous heavy alcohol consumption.

Cyndie has always had a good heart and still does. She went down a rabbit hole and made some bad choices. Lord knows I've also made some bad decisions in the past, as I've already shared. I believe she always knew that keeping the kids at home with me was the best for them and didn't fight me on it. I always wanted the best for her. She is the mother of my children, who are my greatest blessings and she was one of my great loves. A few years later, I was talking to my dad when he mentioned, "Cyndie really broke your heart, didn't she?" Yes, she did, but I always want to look forward, not back.

My focus was on taking care of our kids and getting my job back on track. It all hit me one night after all the kids went to sleep. I remember sitting on our cold concrete patio in the backyard, it was a chilly, damp October night and just crying. How am I going to manage working and taking care of the kids? In hindsight what appeared to be a bad day, bad situation and bad place may have been the second most important day of my life, first one being the day I was born (*Mark Twain*). It gave me greater purpose and along with more empathy for those around me that may be going through life's challenges.

Burtronics Christmas Party

Cyndie and Mike (and Allie)

Wedding in Corona CA

George holding Nick

Cyndie, Allie and George

Cyndie with Samantha

Proud Grandma Pat

93

Allie and George at Halloween

Grandma Irene marrying Bob in Lake St. Louis

Nancy, Jeff and George in Hawaii

Allie, Nick and Grandma Pat

Samantha and Paul

Pool Party fun

New Palm Desert House

All the kids on that teal
green styling carpet

Cyndie and Samantha

Rick, Emma, George and Mike watching football

Hanging out on the front porch

New Yucaipa House

Grandma Irene and Bob

Nick fishing with Grandpa Carl

Samantha and Harlee

Chapter 5

The 2000's - Regrouping & New Opportunities

WHEN ALL THIS HAPPENED with Cyndie, I had to share the situation with my parents, my dad flew from North Carolina to California without me even asking and helped me. He came to take care of Allie, Nick, Samantha and Darby. We also had significant credit card debt that I now had to deal with. If I went bankrupt, that would have impacted my credit and consequently my options to secure any future loans. Unknown to me at that time my good credit would play a major role in an upcoming business venture.

I was very open with Tom, my boss throughout this situation. I explained the challenge of being a full-time dad while also managing my several divisions at Burtronics. As I mentioned in my introduction, there are some situations in your life that you have no control over, you just have to do your best to manage them. Perk and Tom's solution to help was to have Burtronics pay for a nanny, which was very generous. In hindsight, it was also a wise business decision and well worth it based on what I was contributing to the company's bottom line. So, I started my new reality of life.

My dad helped at home for a month. I knew I needed to find a full-time nanny, so I began interviewing. There were a few applicants; one with perhaps half of her teeth, another who could speak only about forty words of English and then a Gothic girl dressed entirely in black; black lips, clothes, hair and neck tattoos. A side benefit of hiring her was that perhaps the kids could learn some interesting magic spells. None really struck me as a good fit. Out of the blue, Veronica, who worked with me and was a great friend, shared that her daughter, Daneilia was looking for a job while she went to college. She already knew the kids and told me that she would organize her school around the kids and my schedule. She was the answer to my prayers. She picked the kids up from school, helped with homework and took care of them as if they were family. Daneilia helped us for a couple of years. Burtronics paid for her and I ended up buying her a dependable Volkswagen Jetta, her dream car at the time. That was some of the best money that I have ever spent. She now has a beautiful family of her own and is doing great. Veronica was one of my personal and professional pillars. Unfortunately, she had health issues and passed away in 2016.

Getting Back to Life

I was focused on taking care of the kids, advancing my career at Burtronics and getting out of credit card debt. My mom and dad helped me with some money and we lived frugally for about two years to pay off everything, which was important for my peace of mind and our future financial well-being. Of course, I could have just made minimum payments; let's do a little math based on a $50,000 credit card balance at 24% interest and making minimum payments over 25 years, that would be $300,791.07 ($250,791.07 of that is interest). So, if you're ever thinking about just making minimum credit card payments, I would strongly advise against it. In my opinion if you don't pay credit cards off every month you are negatively impacting your future. It's called immediate gratification, which many people do. *You never want to trade your tomorrow for today.*

That's not to say all debt is bad; if you put a Gucci leopard skin purse or a Rolex watch on credit because you have always wanted it but can't come up with the cash it's probably bad debt. Good debt is borrowing money to make money. Example, if you borrow money at 18% and can safely make 32%, then leveraging money can be good and it's how a lot of wealth in America is created. Later in my story this theory will come into play

The kids were doing well in school. I always believed that keeping them in the same school district and neighborhood was very important. I remembered all the schools I went to and how hard it was to acclimate at times. In our small neighborhood of seventeen homes most of our neighbors had lived there since the houses were built and everyone knew each other. They would occasionally bring us food and offer to take the kids to school and church. The saying "it takes a village" rings so true. Most evenings we would all sit down together for dinner without any distractions, no TV, no phones or hats and would talk about what happened that day among other things.

I also quickly realized that I wasn't the butler and everyone needed to do their fair share around the house. All the kids learned how to do their own laundry, get ready for school, wash dishes, and clean the floors and bathrooms. I went up to Home Depot and bought stepstools, then strategically placed them around the house so that they could be self-sufficient. On Saturday morning there was a "to-do" list, you were not allowed to leave the house or do any fun stuff until you completed your tasks. A well-oiled machine, if I do say so myself.

Many nights after putting the kids to bed I would catch a little shut-eye, then wake up in the early morning hours, around 3 or 4am to get work done. Every now and then people would ask me why I was emailing them at such an odd time. Well, that's when I'm most productive and have no distractions, so I can get a lot done. *Productivity is not a matter of how much time you spend working, it's how much you get done.*

Doing Business

For the most part, Burtronics was a good place to work. After getting back on track I was making more money than ever, and all my divisions were thriving. I probably hired and fired more people than any other manager in the company, but I also believed that I provided more opportunities to individuals. Some people were simply not the right fit, while others essentially fired themselves. After assembling the right team members in the appropriate positions, there was minimal turnover and my teams excelled as fantastic sales machines. My lesson from George at Deutsch about the "the right fit" had made sense and finally stuck with me.

It's hard to let people go sometimes. Tom would say, "firing someone impacts not only them but also their family," and I took that to heart. With that said, there was a job to do. Salespeople are simply either making you money or costing you money. Even if they are making money, someone who is disruptive to the team may still have to go. There were some memorable moments.

One time, I had to terminate a salesperson after he physically assaulted another employee. Jeff was a young guy, about 6'3" and 230 pounds, with a quick temper. It was Friday afternoon and we had heated words behind closed doors in my office. I handed him his final paycheck and showed him out. On the following Monday morning I walked into the office and to my surprise he was at his desk wearing a suit and tie. "Jeff, I thought I terminated you last week?" His response was, "As long as I'm here, you need to pay me." Then he stood up and challenged me, "Why don't you make me leave?" We were in the sales bullpen with about twenty people watching and you could hear a pin drop. I thought this is not going to be pretty, what can I do to diffuse this situation? So, I quickly came up with an idea, I said, "Jeff please stay, that's your choice…in fact let me get you a cup of coffee." Then, I turned to Meg, my secretary and loudly asked her to call the San Bernardino police, "and inform them that there is a trespasser here who may be violent." As she did, I brought him a cup of coffee and simply said, "Make yourself comfortable." I don't think he was expecting that. A couple of minutes later he was out the door, never to be seen again.

Daniel was a good guy and later became a good friend, but I had to let him go due to performance issues. I liked him, but the sales were just not there; he was costing me money. I did something unique with him, I took him out to Starbucks where we had a conversation and I tried to impart some advice before parting ways. To this day, he doesn't appreciate it when I suggest, "let's go to Starbucks for a cup of coffee." It's challenging, but you can't let friendship interfere with your business decisions. It was about getting the job done and being impartial. I didn't care if you were a little green, bisexual, warlock; just get the job done. I had to appear in front of the State Labor Commissioner a few times over the years. I never lost a case; I believe I was a very fair manager. A couple of years later, Daniel returned and expressed an interest in working for me again. He was the first person I ever rehired after being terminated. He shared with me that he didn't like me when I let him go, but now he understood. He had become a better salesperson and appreciated that he always knew where he stood with me. Daniel was the only person I fired once and hired three times; a fact that will become evident as my story unfolds.

Herding Cats, I mean Kids

I feel very fortunate that my kids helped each other and most of the time demonstrated common sense. I also believe that at times they kept each other in check, so I didn't have to as much. My dad on a number of occasions expressed surprise, as he put it; I defied the odds that at least one of them didn't do anything really crazy. I suppose his point of reference was me growing up. Think about having four teenage George's, wouldn't that be fun. One advantage of being the primary parent is that you are the judge, jury and executioner, no appeals process...pretty simple. Another thing was that I heard directly from the people and teachers who were interacting with the kids, without any filters.

One day, I was driving to parent-teacher conferences at Wildwood Elementary. I had four meetings back-to-back, so it was a long day. I remember thinking, "wow, what a pain, spending all day in teacher meetings." But a minute later it hit me, this was probably the best use of my time ever, much better than dealing with work-related matters. I was one of the few fathers who would attend those conferences. It was important to hear firsthand how the kids were doing, along with building relationships with their teachers. Later that year, the principal called me and said she wanted to talk to me. When my mom received calls like that, it was never a good thing. I went in that day and she said that I would be a great asset to the Site Council, which oversees how money is spent at the school. Well, sign me up. I was on the Site Council for the next two years. Later, I joined the PTA, which provided me with more valuable insights into the school's operations. In 2003, I was awarded PTA Member of the Year in California. I believe the principal may have influenced the decision and lobbied in my favor; it was truly an honor. Over the years, I came to know many of their teachers, staff and all the principals at every school they attended.

Fun Times for Us

It wasn't all work and no play; my mom and Bob would take the kids to the Midwest for a few weeks every summer where they had a nice house on Lake St. Louis. Nick learned to pilot a small lake boat, while

Allie, Sam and Darby raised baby ducks. They swam, visited museums and cooked. I still have all the photo albums that my mom made every year documenting what they did. Cyndie remarried and was doing well. She became a big part of the kids' lives and also helped me with them. One year, we went on a houseboat trip with Jeff and Nancy, along with their daughters Sara and Jenny. By the way, the mosquitos at that Arkansas lake were large enough to carry you away. We visited Las Vegas, Northern California, the Grand Canyon, North Carolina, Alaska and Mexico. I had to work a lot but tried to squeeze in some fun time with the kids.

Business…the Good, the Bad and the Ugly

In 2004, the owner of Burtronics, Perk decided to retire and sell the company to an ESOP (Employee Stock Ownership Plan), theoretically transferring ownership to the employees with a bank financing most of the sale. On the front end it looked like a great thing, but it turned out to be nearly the death of the company. Perk returned about five years later and ousted Tom after the company went from ninety-eight employees to less than twenty; it was essentially on life support by then.

About the only thing that I didn't enjoy at Burtronics was a couple of my counterparts who managed the other sales teams, namely Gabe and Larry. Conflict started when I returned to the San Bernardino office. They were self-proclaimed Christians who volunteered to help me train my salespeople. I'm not overly religious, but I'm a big believer in the Golden Rule "In everything, do to others what you would have them do to you" which to me is a fundamental ethical principle. Having them help sounded good, but during the introduction at the first training, Larry said, "The customer will never care about you or your family. Your job is to maximize profit. You don't need to care about them or theirs." That's not what I believed in. I always felt that business should be a win-win situation, so I pulled my people out and conducted my own training from that point on.

Gabe was initially a good guy who helped me at the beginning of my sales career. He was one of my go-to guys when I had questions, until Larry came into the picture. They wanted to hold prayer meetings in the office that excluded women and "non-believers." I opposed this idea; I felt the office was not an appropriate place for such exclusions or religion. They even told one of my salespeople from India, Madu, that he would never be successful because he wasn't a Christian, which to say the least upset him. When I asked them if they really said that and why, their response was "yes, because it's the truth." Maybe it was their truth, but in my view not "the truth."

I believe the final straw for them was when I proposed opening an office in Temecula, a rapidly growing area. They had been working in that area for the last five years and had only made a few copier placements, I think it was about eight. I asked Tom to let me open an office, he did and they spun big time. At one point I asked them, "Would you rather Burtronics win business down there or Sharp, Canon, Xerox?" Larry said, "I'm not answering that question." Well, in my opinion, that was an answer. That office turned out to be very successful.

In late 2004 Gabe and I were equal managers. Tom, in his wisdom said that whoever had the highest sales numbers in the last quarter would be promoted to Vice President. In my opinion, that was not the right way to build a team; it only served to widen the gap between us. Gabe's team ended up outperforming mine because Larry had secured a large copier order from the San Manuel Casino. Burtronics ordered equipment and was ready to deliver the systems, but the customer discovered that they had paid over the retail price. Furthermore, I believe Larry had manipulated the numbers provided to the customer. Consequently, they canceled the order leaving Burtronics with about a quarter-million-dollars' worth of copiers in the warehouse. It was a bad situation that created a major cash flow problem for the company. You may be able to deceive a customer once but when they discover the truth, they will never do business with you again. The following week, I contacted Loretta, the CFO at Mark Christopher Chevrolet and scheduled a meeting with my sales representative, Ed and me. I specifically told Ed not to speak when I asked a closing question, no matter what! It's like playing tennis; you hit the ball over the net and they need to return it. The one who speaks first loses. That's a sales rule, right? I approached the sale during our meeting with mini agreements. Tommy Hopkins would have been proud of me. At the appropriate time I pulled out a sales order to replace all their copiers in all three locations, placed it on her desk, then set a pen on top of the order and said, "It makes sense. I would do it." Then turned the order around towards her and shut up. After a long minute of staring, Loretta said, "you're good" and signed the order. We walked out with a large order. Ed had a significant commission, and all of our problematic inventory was placed. The following year, I was promoted to Vice President. To me, my paycheck and doing a good job was always more important than a title or trophy.

At the end of the day, I was tired of fighting battles with my competitors and then coming into the office to fight battles with Gabe and Larry. If I said black, they wanted white. By the way, thank you guys; that eventually motivated me to make a change.

Here's a life lesson to take to heart; just because someone else does something bad doesn't give you the justification to do bad stuff also. The short of it is that some people try to rationalize their actions based on things other people do or have been done to them. Two wrongs don't make a right. Wrong is wrong so *you cannot justify doing something bad no matter what has been done to you, if it's wrong then it's wrong!* I always wished them the best for them no matter what they wished me…but karma is a bitch.

Going, Going, Gone

It was 2006, and I had just experienced my most successful year at Burtronics. I had built great sales teams and was earning more money than ever before. The RISO company contacted me and asked if I wanted to go to the Super Bowl. We had become one of their top dealers in North America. Not bad for a product we were getting ready to kick to the curb back in the 90's. The Seahawks and Steelers were playing, and the Rolling Stones performed at halftime. What a blast! RISO did everything first-class. I had dinner with a couple of Hall of Fame players, and I even had a beer with Peyton Manning. He told me he was going to win the Super Bowl the next year, which he did. The Steelers won that year, it was a great, memorable experience.

About that time, I was approached by Debbie, a representative for a drinking water purification company called Pure Health Solutions Incorporated (PHSI). I was the go-to guy at that time for introducing new programs and products at Burtronics. I wasn't interested at first, but Debbie was persistent so I started researching the water market and what PHSI had to offer. I analyzed water revenue data, market growth, competitors and even visited a couple of their dealers at my own expense. One of them was Marc in Phoenix. Marc is a great guy and we hit it off. I still talk to Marc, along with taking motorcycle rides and hooking up with him when I'm in Phoenix or he's in Dana Point. Craig, the owner of PHSI had designed the PW1R water system. I believe it's one of the best drinking water systems ever made, I still have one in our kitchen. One day he contacted me directly after Debbie had been hounding me for a couple of months. Craig shared with me that they knew who I was from the business machine industry and that they were searching for a distributor in Southern California. Therefore, he wanted to fly in and meet me in person. I said, "Craig, I don't know if I'm your guy. I still drink out of the garden hose." His response was, "It doesn't matter what you do. It matters what everyone else is doing and everyone is buying bottled water now, we have a better way," it made sense. Craig came out and we met at the Mission Inn in Riverside. We had dinner and a few drinks...okay, maybe more than a few. Craig was a smart, interesting, fun, creative and athletic guy who simply drank a little too much and had a tendency to get into altercations. Never a boring moment with him. Craig sold his business in 2010 and passed away in 2021 at the age of fifty-eight. I believe drinking may have played a role in his passing. I always share with soon-to-be-retired friends that you need projects and hobbies when you stop working for a living. Drinking every day is not a good retirement plan.

The more I thought about it, the more I started considering taking the PHSI water system and starting a new company myself. So, I developed a business plan. I always made plans for new products and offices, so this wasn't something new for me. Burtronics had been fertile ground, providing me with hands-on experience in opening new offices along with launching new products and services. As I mentioned, there was ongoing conflict between Gabe, Larry and me. Perk was out of the picture; Tom was in charge but was not managing things very effectively. This was my chance to do my own thing and implement all the ideas I had but couldn't pursue at Burtronics. You'll never get rich or in my case, fully fulfilled until you have your own show.

After seventeen and a half years, on April 1, 2006 (yes, April Fool's Day), I went into Tom's office and handed him my resignation. By the way, Tom liked my plan so much he ended up investing $50,000 in the new company, Pure Water Technology Inc.

I also gave my business plan to a few other people. I always have found it beneficial to get perspectives, views and honest feedback. Sometimes you can get tunnel vision when you're working on an idea or project. Many times, people will tell you how great your plan sounds even though they wouldn't invest a dime. I wanted to hear any downsides they see and what could go wrong...so bring it on, you're not going to hurt my feelings. I just didn't want to go broke or waste my time with a bad plan or investment. *Time is the most valuable thing you will ever have in life.* One person I gave it to was Mike, my former brother-in-law and he read it with his wife, Laure. Laure told Mike that if anyone could make this a success, George could. Mike ended up quitting his job and working with me. Mike started on straight commission, an independent contractor at the beginning, that's how much he believed in the company.

One night, I sat the kids down and explained my plan to start Pure Water Technology (PWT). It was like talking to them in Chinese, I know they didn't really understand and grasp the risk involved. They had never had to sleep in a car, of course I had. I guess they had faith in me, so after explaining my plan the next question I believe Nick asked was, "now, can we go out and play?"

I was confident that I had a good plan, so I jumped in with both feet. In the words of Zig Ziglar... *"Confidence is going after Moby Dick in a rowboat and taking tartar sauce with you."*

Starting my Start-up

Employee number #001 was Eddie, responsible for installations and service. Eddie turned out to be a hardworking and loyal guy. He embraced many of my business and personal philosophies wholeheartedly. Initially he would call me with questions, some were simple and I would say "you're the manager, you don't have to call me just make the decision." I believe he was concerned about making a mistake. My personal take on mistakes are; *embrace mistakes, and learn from them, if you're not making mistakes then you're probably not doing enough.* It's ok to screw something up every now and then. He said he never had a boss like me, which I took as a compliment. I never liked micromanaging the people who worked with me and I believe most of them appreciated that.

We set up our shop in the back of my neighbor's Payday Advance in Redlands for $700 a month. More than once in the first few months, I thought, "was this a mistake?" I started the business with $100,000 and had taken a $200,000 Home Equity Line of Credit (HELOC) loan on my house before leaving Burtronics. I assumed that after leaving Burtronics no one would lend me a dime without any income and starting a new business, so that was my backup money. I believe if you create a business plan that is 70% to 80% correct, you're a genius. One of my flaws was undercapitalization, so the HELOC money ended up being very important.

In less than three months, Tom asked if he could start withdrawing $5,000 per month from the company. It's important to note that I had no salary and was not taking any money out of the company at that time myself. I asked why, he said he was building a new house and needed the money. Within an hour, I was at Burtronics in his office with a $50,000 check from my HLOC home loan and paperwork stating that after repaying him, he would own zero percent of the company. He was a short-term thinker or maybe he was just nervous about opening up a multi-million business in the back of a seedy Payday Advance store…I know this is far reaching comparison but Apple started in a garage and last time I check they were doing ok. That $50,000 investment in PWT would have been worth millions a few years later. On a side note, once I was told by Dan Caldwell, cofounder of Tapout Inc. Clothing, to always pay yourself first; well that was never my philosophy and it may have damaged the business when we had challenging moments. There were times that I didn't receive a paycheck in order to take care and retain my employees. To me it would be like Captain Smith jumping on the first lifeboat when the Titanic was going down. By the way Captain Smith will be also included later in my story after buying a boat.

In life, you come to crossroads, and I believe I have traveled down some rough, dusty, bad roads. However, at the major crossroads I think I've been lucky or smart enough to choose the correct path. Getting Tom out probably saved the company in the long run.

Quite a few of the employees left Burtronics soon after my departure. Most of them came to me looking for a job, but I made a promise to Gabe and Tom that I wouldn't damage Burtronics by recruiting or hiring anyone. Daniel would always pop into our shabby little PWT Payday Advance office and would ask me to hire him. Finally, he said it's crazy at Burtronics and he was leaving no matter what. He said that if I cared about him and his family, I would hire him…so I did. On his final day, Gabe found out he was going to PWT and I believe shared with him that he would rather have him go to Xerox, Canon, Sharp or any of his direct competitors than me. In my opinion, that was stupid and crazy, that would have created much more damage to Burtronics. When I talked to Tom and Gabe later that week, I shared that I had kept my word and turned away quite a few other Burtronics employees who had approached me. This situation and the demise of the company was 100% their own doing. They needed to look in the mirror.

Mike and Daniel became bedrocks of PWT. They were always hitting the ball out of the park, securing placements in major accounts. They helped develop our systems, training and marketing. As I have already shared, I would at times question myself, "did I do the right thing by leaving a secure job and steady paycheck for this new venture," as any sane person would. They were always the voices of positivity and encouragement. It turned out to be a great decision to share my business plan with Mike and to hire Daniel for the third time. Eddie, Brian and a few other people were also key to PWT's success, I surrounded myself with great people.

Later that year, I understood Larry had a major meltdown because I sent him, along with all the other managers at Burtronics, a Christmas card saying, "Hope you have a great 2007." A Christmas card, really? I still had ESOP stock in Burtronics, so if they did well it would have also benefited me. It never crossed my mind that wishing them well at Christmas would be a problem. Just shows how far down the rabbit hole they had gone. Remember what I said about holding a grudge is like holding a piece of hot coal in your hands; their hands had third-degree burns. So now that I was out of the picture, Gabe, Larry and their following should have done great, right? About a year after I left, they ended up creating significant damage to the company. Many employees had left, along with the departure of major customers. Caring more about profit than your customers is never a good business strategy in my opinion. As I have already shared my philosophy was to do a good job for your customers and the money will follow. They also created a major divide between Sales and Service/Administration; you simply can't operate a successful company like that. Compounding the problem, Tom was an absentee leader. In just over a year the once-thriving company had dwindled to less than half its former size and was still losing business. Eventually, my vested Burtronics ESOP company stock, which was almost $400,000 on paper, evaporated and become worthless; I never saw a dime.

I was focused on PWT, trying to figure out what our most profitable markets were and how to position our product/service. We decided to concentrate on commercial, not residential. Businesses install multiple systems, making them easier to service and manage. Systems were placed as rentals versus outright selling the systems. Rentals provide ongoing residual income and better value the company. Similar to the revenue model of a cable TV company. It may seem obvious, but I assure you it wasn't. One of the main challenges of this model is cash flow. You need to finance the new placements or have a pile of cash since you're not profitable for about two years after an installation due to the initial cost of equipment and expenses.

The Crash of 2009

Initially PWT was selling the customer/equipment contracts, which means installing systems and then receiving a lump sum of discounted money from finance companies or banks to hold the equipment title and collect monthly payments until the agreements reached their term. That was key to providing enough cash flow in order to grow. I believe that in business, you're either growing or shrinking; there is no staying the same. In 2009 the economy tanked, causing the finance companies and banks to stop lending money/financing agreements. We had orders but no way to purchase systems to install them; our cash flow was severely impacted. We were at a crossroads, perhaps it was time to double down.

I contacted Grant; I knew him because he had helped Craig secure funding to start PHSI. We met at Big Canyon Country Club in Newport Beach, where I shared our cash flow challenge. He asked how much I needed, I said two million would do the trick. Later that week, I had paperwork in front of me for a $2,000,000 loan to draw on at 18% interest and a $5,000 monthly management fee. My dad thought I was crazy. But two things went through my mind. First, if I took the loan at 18%, I believed I could make 32% on it. So, we would still be positive if my calculations were correct. Second, if I owe you $50,000, it's my problem; if I owe you $2,000,000, it's yours. This enabled PWT to acquire another struggling company and continue making placements. Sometimes when everyone else is retreating, it's a prime time to charge ahead and that's exactly what we did. A quote from Warren Buffet that I think somewhat applies is *"Buy when there's blood in the street, even if the blood is yours"*

About a year later as financial institutions started loosening their purse strings. I created an updated business plan that included our customers, market data, revenue and forecasts then had it bound. It was almost an inch thick and I started cold-calling banks. Remember when I mentioned that my parents said I always had a knack for knocking on doors? Well, that talent really came in handy.

We were into Grant for $1,278,000 by then. A Small Business Loan (SBA) would pay off Grant, thus greatly reducing our operating costs and allowing us to run much of the business by now using the established revenue from current placements to fund further growth. After talking to half dozen or more banks, US Bank listened, asked a lot of questions and approved PWT for a loan. I met Grant at Maestro's in Crystal Cove with a bottle of Opus One wine and bought him a steak. Then shared with him that all the money had been wired back into his account and I was terminating our agreement. "Grant, thanks for your help, isn't it great that you received all your money back and made a good profit?" Grant said, "thanks, but I was really happy with making 18% on my money." I bet he was. Grant is a good businessman and a great guy; he would later assist me in selling Pure Water Technology and we still have lunch every now and then.

Family Picture 2001

Fun with Nick

Daneilia an answer to my prayers

Girls in Lake St Louis with ducks

George and Jeff riding though the Rockies

Kids having fun with aunt Veronia

Rebuilt and painted in the garage by me

Jeff, Terry and George catching dinner

Red Brady GT kit car build and painted by me...it's good to have projects

Allie's first car and Christmas present 2006

Carl and Carol's house in the country

Grandpa Carl and Carol visiting us in Yucaipa

Super Bowl 2006

PWT first office, what a dump!

George's drawing, made it on a
flight to meet Marc

Flying with Paul in Chesterfield

Grandma Irene on thier boat in Lake St. Louis

We are in the news

113

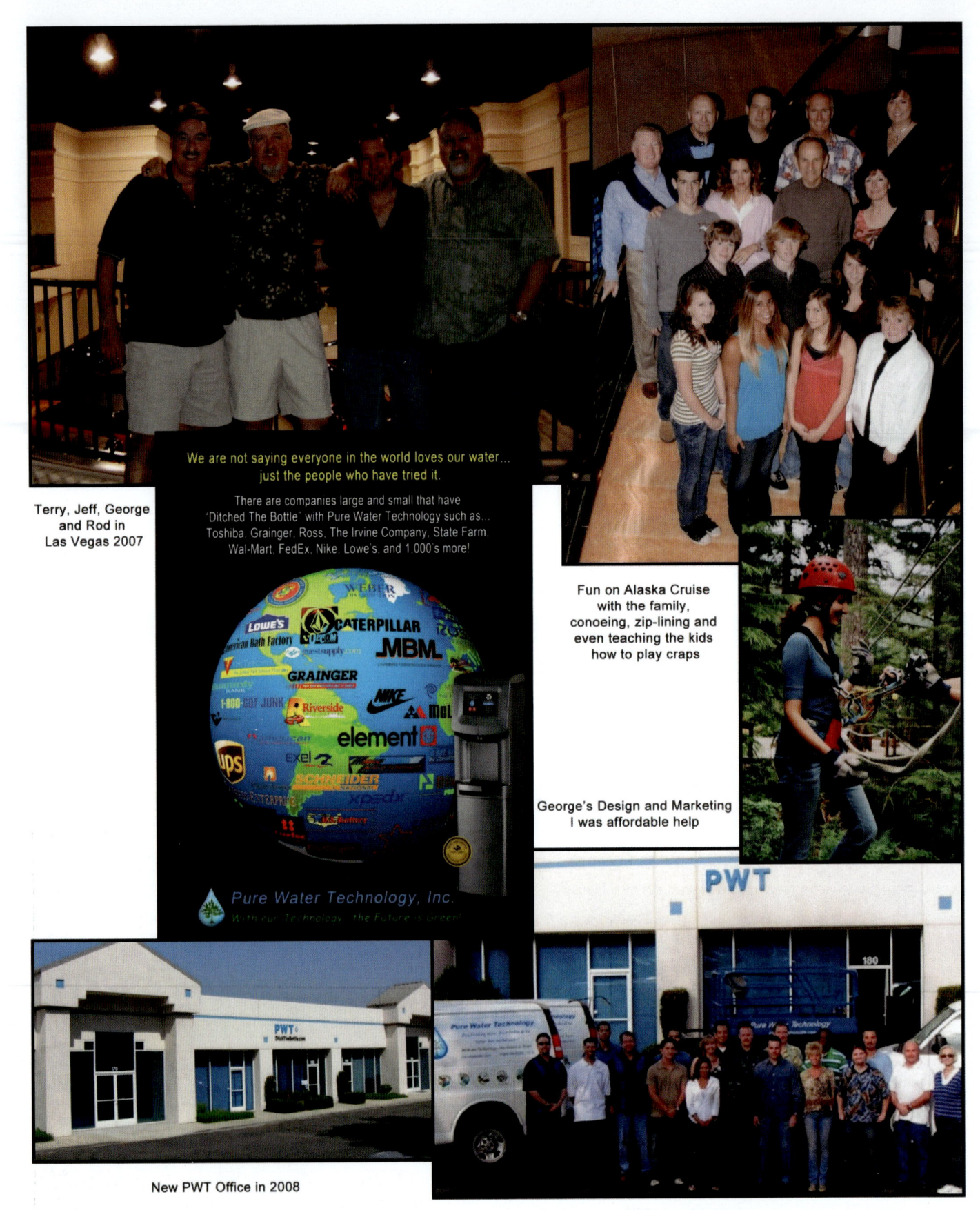

We are not saying everyone in the world loves our water...
just the people who have tried it.

There are companies large and small that have
"Ditched The Bottle" with Pure Water Technology such as...
Toshiba, Grainger, Ross, The Irvine Company, State Farm,
Wal-Mart, FedEx, Nike, Lowe's, and 1,000's more!

Terry, Jeff, George
and Rod in
Las Vegas 2007

Fun on Alaska Cruise
with the family,
conoeing, zip-lining and
even teaching the kids
how to play craps

George's Design and Marketing
I was affordable help

New PWT Office in 2008

The PWT Team

114

Chapter 6

The 2010's - Growing, Selling, Retiring, Love & Adventure

AS THE ECONOMY REBOUNDED PWT WAS THRIVING, we were securing placements at major companies such as Costco, Union Pacific, Ross, Walmart along with many others. I think I had the right people in the right positions. You never want your linebacker playing quarterback, so evaluating and positioning talent is very important. I compared PWT organizationally to a stool with three legs; Service, Sales and Administration, all very important. Communicate effectively, focus on your job and don't stress about the others. But, if one of the legs of the stool fails it affects all of us.

We were a happy place to work at and I didn't have to micromanage people, it felt nice. Along with having the right people you need good systems. So, I was very active in creating systems to help my employees succeed and grow. Also, I developed most of our marketing materials, which was a fun part of the business for me. I'll share some of those in a minute, but life is not all business, there is more.

Dating and Relationships

At first, I thought, "Who would want to date a guy with four young kids?" Well, it seems that sometimes taking care of the kids may have earned me brownie points and I believe that I'm a fun, happy and optimistic guy. There's a tombstone/sign in the pet cemetery on Catalina Island that says, "George, He Was Happy and Playful." Not bad, simple and to the point.

I've always enjoyed spending time with friends, girlfriends and people in general, sharing life experiences. So, I dated when I had time between work, school, the kid's activities and my responsibilities.

There were a few longer-term relationships such as Alisa, she already had three kids and wanted more, which was a deal breaker. Don't get me wrong I love my kids, but I'd rather eat a light bulb at that point in my life then have any more kids. Then there was a few that were just one date and done. I jumped on Match.com, because it was challenging to meet new people while being at home with the kids, so let's go online.

I remember one date, we agreed to meet across from the Mission Inn in Riverside. Her Match profile looked good. When she walked in, I didn't recognize her. The picture I saw on-line was not current and the lighting must have been way better, it was false advertising. Not being a totally superficial person, I felt obligated to at least buy her a drink and talk.

A few minutes into the conversation, she mentioned she had two kids; well, I have four, so no big deal. One of them was a little slow because he was a "digger," a term I wasn't familiar with at that time. I understand he may be slow because he ate a lot of glue or got hit in the head with a baseball...but a digger, do tell? So, she explained that whenever they went out, her son loved to dig in the dirt and sand. Once, I had a dog that was a digger, he didn't last long. This wasn't good, I had always maintained a beautiful yard so inviting her family over for a barbecue was now out of the question. She continued to tell the story of what happened and how he was deprived of oxygen. This is what I came across:

ABC News - Teen Rescued after Sand Tunnel Collapses

Aug. 4, 2011- A day at the beach turned into terror for a Newport Beach, Calif., teen who became trapped when the oversized sand hole he was digging with a friend caved in on him.

"I thought I was going to die," Matt said in an interview with NBC News from Orange, Calif., Thursday. "I was just really scared. I didn't know if anyone could hear me when I was screaming for help."

Suddenly, the tunnel caved in and collapsed on the one boy completely burying him under the sand. One family member alerted the lifeguard while other beachgoers immediately jumped in and began digging with any utensils available on the beach.

Dirk Vanderwall was among those that darted towards the boy to help the rescue effort.

"It was very frantic," Vanderwall told ABC affiliate KABC. "We knew somebody was buried there. We didn't know how old the person was. But as we kept digging it was longer and longer, it took a long time, you just start thinking it couldn't be going well."

Fire fighters pulled up the boy alive after 30 minutes of digging.
Footage shows the crowd erupting with cheers as the boy emerges alive and is taken to a nearby hospital where he was treated.

Of course, my next logical question was, "does he still dig?" "Yes, sometimes, but he's more careful now." At that point, she went to the restroom. The bartender was listening in and we just did a long, long, long look at each other. Soon after he gave me the check, I paid and excused myself. I just wasn't digging that date...I know, bad pun.

I dated Cyndi II for about four years. We met at PWT, she was a sales representative and pretty good at her job. Dating an employee is probably not recommended by most Human Resources Directors, but I did it anyway. Cyndi II was nice, had two boys, but from the beginning I noticed that her parenting style was different from mine. Something you should be aware of if you ever blend families. My kids were doing their own laundry and cleaning the house in grade school, while she was still sometimes cutting up their food at dinner when they were in their teens. One night, we were sitting on the back porch in Yucaipa and she asked, "when the kids go to college, are we moving in together?" It was a very valid question, but it caught me off guard. Well, I don't know. I realized she was not "the one" and I was wasting her time. The next night, I broke up with her and she took it pretty hard. She was good, but just not the right fit for me. I believe I did her a favor, similar to what George at Deutsch had done for me twenty years earlier, but she probably didn't see it that way at the time. Years later, she would get married, have another baby and I always wished her a happy life.

By the way, my dad later said, "You dodged a bullet with her." He seldom said anything negative, so I asked him, "Why didn't you say anything earlier?" His response was a life lesson that I still try to use today. *"If a person doesn't ask for advice they probably aren't going to listen."*

Growing PWT

At PWT, I was busy creating systems and working with banks to help continue to grow the business. One important system was our Customer Relationship Management (CRM) software based on a program called QuickBase. I taught myself how to customize it by writing code and programing it for sales and service. It was something that I had wanted to implement at Burtronics for a long time, but I always faced obstacles. In my opinion, it was crucial for effectively operating and expanding our business. Now that I was making the calls, I could make it happen. It took me over a year to build it and I continued to fine-tune it over the next few years. I think it was a great tool, even better than Salesforce and other commercial programs because it was tailored to PWT along with incorporating my sales methods and philosophies. Since it was remotely cloud based you could access the program anywhere through an iPad to input data and retrieve useful account information. I believe I understood the needs of sales managers and what salespeople would embrace. It had measurable next steps, information on deals that were won and lost to aid in future marketing along with simple ways to organize suspects, prospects and customers.

I created our logo, website, email portal and domain, "DitchTheBottle.com." Then we incorporated attention grabbing marketing videos such as one showing me blowing apart competitive water coolers with a

12-gauge shotgun and another where I'm dropping 5-gallon water bottles off a 32-foot scissor lift and watching them explode. I also developed a service call portal and an online store. A few years later I would delegate this work to a professional company, but I still enjoyed being involved.

While Eddie was on vacation, I filled in for him as the Service Manager. I've always been a hands-on guy and I believe it's beneficial to have a firsthand understanding of how things work in the real world. I started receiving twenty to thirty phone calls a day requesting service. When Eddie returned, I asked him if this was normal and how he managed to get anything else done. Yep, it was normal. So, I redesigned the service tags on the front of the systems to include a QR code and our website. This modification directed service requests to our website. In just a couple of months, over ninety percent of service was being requested through to our website portal for our technicians to complete. This approach was significantly more effective because it provided a firsthand account of the service issue directly from the customer, while also eliminating the need to hire a full-time service dispatcher to handle answering calls and logging service requests. It's always better and more cost-effective to automate than to hire.

Marketing was a fun job for me. I created blogs, videos, ads and other activities that were crucial in keeping PWT on the first page of Google. I personally designed ads for trade publications, email blasts and postcard mailers. My philosophy was that a low-tech 6" x 9" postcard would be a good way to communicate our message. You don't have to open it, and it would be handled by multiple people in an organization. Sometimes the CEO would be the decision-maker, while other times the receptionist that was just tired of loading 42-pound bottles of water on the cooler would contact us. One of our very successful postcard/marketing campaigns was called "Meet Pete," which featured our water cooler dressed up in various outfits such as Business Pete, Safety Pete, Health Pete and Green Pete. Pete communicated customer benefits in a simple, engaging way that captured attention. Sales Rule #7, if you're keeping track, the first thing you need to do in a sale or meeting is to grab your audience's attention. We would mail fifteen thousand marketing pieces every two weeks, four times a year for our annual or semi-annual marketing campaigns. Now, the big question: why "Meet Pete?" We wanted to introduce a new solution for providing water to employees and it simply rhymes. No high dollar marketing research needed for that one.

One of my jobs at Burtronics was to assist customers with printing documents, essentially creating paper and we had an abundance of paper at Burtronics. To me, this felt like one step away from using clay tablets. I wanted to minimize paper, so I created a marketing presentation for the salespeople on the iPad. We provided iPads to everyone. Agreements and other documents were signed, transferred and all stored electronically. All service calls were dispatched and logged on the iPad. I had fun learning and developing these technologies along with getting creative to grow PWT. Guess that college semester as an art major came in handy sometimes.

Beach Life and Meeting New Friends

I had rented a house on the Newport Beach peninsula for nine months. Living on the beach was fun, but that area was primarily comprised of about 80% short-term weekly party rentals. I quickly found out that was not the place that I wanted to put down roots. Also, as the kids were leaving the nest, I knew the Inland Empire was not where I wanted to spend the rest of my life either. The next place I rented was in Corona Del Mar (CDM), known as the Crown of the Sea. Not only it had weather great, the people were friendly and very active. There were plenty of parties, fantastic bars, restaurants and music. Once, I was having lunch at a restaurant called the Red O, a girl sitting next to me mentioned she was from the East Coast and had observed that everyone here was happy and friendly. Then she asked me why? I said, "The weather is great year-round, people have money, there's always fun stuff to do and everyone for the most part are healthy and active. If you can't be happy here, you're not going to be happy anywhere." That's truly how I felt about the California Coast.

One night I went to a CDM neighborhood party where I met Kim and Victoria. Victoria appeared lively and fun, so I decided to ask for her number and planned to invite her to a hockey game the following day. When I first called to ask her to go, she said "no, I don't even know you." My response was, "I'm asking you out so we can get to know each other." Then she said no because she had plans to go out with her girlfriends that night. "Well, luckily, it's a day game, so I'll have you back by five. I'll come pick you up, can I have your address?" Her response was "I don't want you stalking me." I gave her my address and saw her at noon that day. I guess at that point she just ran out of "no's."

We jumped in my car and after just a few minutes on the highway, she said, "I never want to work again and I have my own money." Then, "I have a heart condition; my doctor says I may live for thirty days or thirty years." Well, *tomorrow is never promised*, so that didn't faze me. We had a great time. I found out later that after our date she shared with Kim, "I may have a new boyfriend."

After about four dates, I invited her over to watch *Sons of Anarchy*, a popular TV show about a biker gang. She loved to ride motorcycles. We were settling in with our pajamas on, it was 9 o'clock and the show was about to start when someone knocked on my back door. Nobody ever came to my back door. As I opened the door there stood Catherine, an ex-girlfriend who I had broken up with a few weeks earlier. As their eyes locked on each other, I found myself in the middle, feeling like laser beams were burning through me. Catherine let out a scream. Victoria jumped up, grabbed her stuff and shot out the door. I couldn't stop her. After calming Catherine down and confirming the breakup once more, she left. Victoria wouldn't answer my calls, but I knew she owned a clothing boutique and was planning to be there in the morning. Just to be clear, I'm not a stalker, but I'm also not a quitter…guess there's a fine line there. That morning, I bought flowers at Browne's in CDM. Then I thought that might not be enough, so I went back home and borrowed a baseball bat from my neighbor, Robert. When I walked into her store, I held out both hands; flowers in my right hand and a bat in my left. I said, "It's not my fault. I can explain. You can whack me with the bat if you want or take the flowers. I would prefer you choose the second option," she laughed and took the flowers. I quickly returned the bat to my car.

By the way, Catherine was Asian, which will become relevant in another story. I once asked out of ignorance whether someone was Asian or Oriental. I quickly found out Oriental was a rug, not a person.

Victoria was a social butterfly who had been living on the coast for most of her life and knew a lot of people. Many of my current friends, or as Maddie calls them the "Crew," I met through her. She took me over to Jeff and Val's on Christmas Eve and we had a blast. After dating for a few months, I was booted from my CDM house because the owner wanted to convert it into an Airbnb. As I mentioned before, I had always liked Laguna Beach. I had stopped in there twenty years ago with Hooter and thought what a great place. Now, let's move to Laguna Beach!

Laguna Beach, Surfs Up

Laguna Beach has over 100 restaurants and bars, attracting tourists from around the world. With attractions such as The Pageant of the Masters, Sawdust Festival, Art Walk, and beautiful beaches, it's a fun and picturesque destination. On one summer day, I counted over 20 live bands playing around town. I moved into an apartment right in the middle of the action; it was just a few hundred feet from downtown. I could hear the music at night and waves hitting the beach in the morning.

One Friday night, Victoria, Jeff, Valerie and I went to Laguna Sushi. About halfway through dinner, Victoria turned to me and out of the blue started asking if I wanted to date the Asian waitresses. It turned really ugly, really fast, so we ended up leaving. Then, on the street she continued to have a meltdown. Jeff and Valerie tried to intervene and calm things down with no avail. After a few months and a few drinks, I believe she still couldn't shake the memory of that night with Catherine. At that point, I told her to go home and that I wouldn't argue about something I didn't do or even consider. The next day she sent me an email apologizing. I was still bruised and a bit upset by the whole incident. So, using my twenty-four-hour rule of thinking before talking or acting, I asked her to meet me at Stacks restaurant in Dana Point on Monday morning. I wanted to be with Victoria, but I wasn't going to let this become a recurring theme. I also liked sushi then and still do.

After some thought, I realized that *being right or even justified isn't always the most important thing, as long as you don't compromise your integrity or morals.* So, it really wasn't a matter of winning an argument or proving a point. Maybe a good comparison is a "Pyrrhic Victory." Look it up; it's about a Greek general who wins a victory against the Romans at too great a cost. Sometimes it's not worth it even if you're right. When we met that Monday, I think I surprised her. Without going into the details of what happened, I just asked her what she needed so that this would never happen again. She said she would prefer no communication with Catherine. Later she shared with me that she thought I was there to break up.

I had invested in an Agarwood plantation in Vietnam with Catherine. She would frequently text or email me questions about the business and I was always honest with Victoria about our discussions. I made one call to Catherine while driving away from Stacks that morning and said no more calls, texts or emails. Later, I lost my money in that investment along with a few other people. Catherine was smart, but not a good businessperson. The relationship with Victoria was on solid ground and nothing like that ever happened again.

Victoria and I would travel up north to see Jimmy and Sheila, as well as Darby, Matt and Maddie in Seattle. During our journeys we visited San Francisco where her son lived, we enjoyed motorcycle rides with the American Thunder bike club and went to Las Vegas, where she loved to play Wheel of Fortune slots. After a year filled with fun, meeting new people, enjoying lots of music and dancing, we embarked on a road trip to Vegas because her daughter was hosting a party at the Rio. It was a long week and drove back home on Friday the 13th, 2015. We were worn out, but Victoria, being the energizer bunny, said there's a good band playing at Skyloft and a lot of friends will be there. What about popping over? Well, don't threaten me with a good time; let's do it. We danced until closing, then went back to my apartment and fell fast asleep after a long day.

I woke up at 3 o'clock in the morning and felt a strong breeze blowing through the bedroom window. I got out of bed and closed the window, then touched Victoria; something seemed off. She was warm and appeared to be sound asleep, but something was different. I felt for her pulse and couldn't find it. I remember on our first date she told me about her heart. I moved her to the floor and started CPR compressions, after a few minutes I called 911. Then I called Jeff and Valerie, they arrived at my place in less than fifteen minutes. The paramedics couldn't revive her. We went to Laguna Beach Mission Hospital and around 5 o'clock that morning I called her daughters, Shanna and Chynna with the news. It was one of the hardest calls I have ever made in my life.

Flying Kites and Traveling

PWT was growing, we had good systems and people in place which enabled me to put the business on autopilot at times, giving me the chance to relax and explore. One of the ways I would relax was by flying kites on Laguna's Main Beach a few times a week. What a great way just to chill-out and much cheaper than professional therapy. I also started running with my next-door neighbor, Mark who participated in the Catalina Island Marathon every year. It was my time to get back in shape and refocus.

PHSI, my supplier of water systems had a manufacturing plant in South Korea and invited me to visit it, so I jumped at the opportunity. I went there with several other dealers and they also wanted to explore more of Asia. So, we thought Thailand would also be a great place to visit after Korea, considering it was just 2,151 miles south. In an odd way, it made sense. I had a friend, Newport Mark, he's an experienced traveler and I valued his input so I shared my trip plans with him. Mark is a unique individual who is financially secure and has the luxury of time. In fact, at the onset of the Covid-19 pandemic in 2020, he left the country and has been traveling for the past four years. Mark had an idea for an adventure. Usually, bad ideas start out as "hold my beer and watch this," but this started out as "wouldn't it be interesting to rent motorcycles and ride all over Cambodia?"

I flew to South Korea with John, Jason, Tom, Bob and a couple of other guys. PHSI had everything covered. They put us up in the best hotels, provided great food, took us on a tour of the factory that was manufacturing our water systems and then we visited the Demilitarized Zone (DMZ). I even went into North Korea, took two steps inside, stood there for less than a minute, took a picture and then jumped back. I have a magnet in my garage to prove it. It was an interesting area; South and North Korea engaged in various activities over the years just to provoke each other. In the 80s, the South erected a 323-foot-tall flagpole on the border. So, North Korea responded by building an even taller one, 525 feet tall, which is the tallest in the world. South Korea was very structured; there are even footprints painted on the sidewalks indicating where you need to stand to flag a cab. Maybe too structured for me.

After that, we traveled to Phuket, Thailand and met up with Mark, which was a prelude to heading over to Cambodia. If Seoul is structured and hard-working, Phuket is like a fun-loving aunt who wears a monitored ankle bracelet, has neck tattoos' and no front teeth, but is a real blast to be with. During our brief stay we explored a large animal sanctuary, rode elephants, played with monkeys and I even had a chance to pet a Bengal tiger. What could go wrong? It was great. When you went into town, especially on the main street called Bangla you always felt you needed to be on guard and aware of people approaching you. At Patong Beach, you could relax and enjoy a cocktail. By the way, that's were a huge tsunami hit in 2004 and wiped out most of the city. It was the deadliest natural disaster in the 21st century, killing 7,400 in Phuket and over 227,000 people in that Indian Ocean area. The hotel on the beach we were at said that everyone staying there was killed. When I asked why there was no memorial and it seemed that everyone was very hesitant to talk about it unless directly asked, they said "it's bad for business." One older local lady I met on the beach said that she was there and saw the water quickly recede, then she tried to warn the people but many tourists ran out to collect sea shells. She quickly hopped on her scooter and headed to high ground. Minutes later a four-story wall of water hit the beach, wiping out everyone there. Now off to Phnom Penh, Cambodia.

Our plan was to fly into Phnom Penh and rented motorcycles for a tour. Our group consisted of two guides, two younger guys from Australia, and then Mark and me. We all rode on 250cc Honda Enduro's with rock-hard seats. The plan was to ride approximately 700 miles in eleven days from Phnom Penh to Angkor Wat Temple and back.

Cambodia was different from Thailand. It wasn't as touristy; the people were nicer and they weren't always trying to extract money from you. But it was also more rural and underdeveloped, which was a direct result of Pol Pot, the Khmer Rouge leader who tried to establish a Communist peasant society. Cities were emptied and his policies resulted in over two million people, 25% of the population being killed between 1975 and 1979. This brutal period in time set the country back by decades. If you were a foreigner, Chinese, Christian or Muslim, you were killed. Wore eyeglasses, were highly educated or fluent in multiple languages, you were killed. If they found a reason to kill one of your family members, the Khmer Rouge didn't want you to get any ideas, so everyone was killed. Before the ride, we had time to visit some interesting places such as "The Killing Fields." Human bones were still floating up to the top of mass grave pits, along with skulls piled 25 feet high. The trees had bark beaten off them because that's where they would swing little kids by their feet, striking the tree to kill them because the Khmer Rouge didn't want to waste bullets. Schools were transformed into torture and re-education camps, complete with detailed records and pictures. It was quite extreme and disturbing to say the least.

On the first day of the ride, we encountered heavy traffic as we left Phnom Penh, just as we had anticipated. One thing you learn quickly are the rules of the road there; anywhere you can fit, it's okay to go. No matter which side of the road, sidewalk or direction of traffic, just go for it. I saw some guy on a scooter get hit by a truck. The ambulance came, asked him a few questions then just left. The onlookers carried him over to the sidewalk after which everyone went about their business. I asked a guy watching with me what just happened and he said the medics ask him if he had any money and when he told them he didn't they drove off. This may be a long eleven days.

On the second day of our trip we ventured into the countryside, where we encountered less traffic but the roads were in bad shape. Sometimes the road would just disappear and then we would ride in open fields. Safer, right? Cambodia has over twenty thousand unexploded landmines from the 1970's and many of the fields we rode through had signs that read "DANGER LANDMINES," a sight not commonly seen in California. The guides warned us that it was very dangerous, but assured us that if we stayed on the trail behind them, we would be safe. That three-legged cow we rode past might beg to differ. At one point I was riding down a muddy path next to a large brush pile when I got too close. A long, 3-inch-thick tree limb speared me in the center of my chest and threw me about 10 feet off the bike. Lucky that I was wearing an armored breastplate or I would have been skewered. We rode next to cliffs with 30-40 feet drops and bamboo bridges that were rebuilt every year after the river flooded and destroyed them. The bridges would shutter and shake under the weight of the motorcycles, it was a bit unnerving.

On the third day, Mark's back tire locked up, pushing him into oncoming traffic and narrowly missing a truck. He was pretty shaken up, so we pulled over to allow him to recover and compose himself. Afterward, we inspected the bike then he traded motorcycles with one of the guides. This wasn't feeling good. That night I started asking the guides some questions; such as how many people have dropped out, been hurt or killed on this ride over the years. The guide shared with me that a guy had fallen off a cliff, the handlebar pierced his chest and he died on a trip this year…so please be careful; you'll probably be okay. As we rode through the towns, you would see hospitals identified by a sign with a red cross. They had large front roll-up garage doors facing the street allowing all the dust from the road to come in. So, if the injury doesn't kill you, the medical treatment may. After gathering a little more information, I calculated that we had about a 50/50 chance of making it through the entire ride unscathed, which in my opinion wasn't good odds. My dad always used to say that I'm a risk taker. He may be right to a certain degree, but I'm a calculated risk taker and prefer the odds in my favor.

The next day, Mark said he wasn't continuing and I agreed. This wasn't the trip we had signed up for, so we left the bikes, commandeered a taxi and headed back to civilization. I read a book about evaluating risk called *IN THIN AIR*. It suggested that *you should assess risk according to your current situation and avoid making decisions based on the time or money already invested.* The book provided an example of climbers on

Mount Everest who died because they continued in bad weather conditions, driven by the significant amount of time and money they had invested in reaching their goal. By the way, the next day one of the young Australians broke his leg and was airlifted to a hospital with one of the guides. Out of the six riders who started the ride, only two managed to finish. Cambodia's wild ride and getting almost kabobbed was life number 8 out of 9. I still want to see the Angkor Wat Temple, but maybe not on a motorcycle. Mark took off to Vietnam and I headed back to California.

The Kids Finding Their Paths

Allie graduated from University California Irvine, but before that she did a foreign exchange program in England then traveled through Europe and met some people from Australian. After finishing college, she went to Australia where she ended up settling down. I flew there and we went scuba diving on the Great Barrier Reef and now have visited a few places there over the years. It's a long flight. She was able to obtain citizenship, has a job as a teacher, ran for city council and married a solid guy, Dan. He even flew 7,185 miles to ask me for my blessing to marry Allie. They now have a little girl, Georgia, my happy granddaughter.

Nick went to Crafton College and worked as an EMT. Then he went to Salt Lake City and for a short time where he became a Mormon and went on a mission, white shirt and all. I didn't think that was a good fit, but as my dad said "believe in your kids and they will figure it out," which he did. After doing that, he went back to college and eventually moved back to Southern California. I always thought he would end up in some kind of technology job since he is great with computers, but he ended up working with people and management. He has always been a people person and has a big heart so that makes sense.

Samantha graduated from California Baptist University, became a nurse which was a good fit for her since she's my little German, very detail oriented. She married Ron and they live in Yucaipa with Isla and Calvin, my bright, smart, active grandkids. Ron is a class act. When they were teenagers, he asked me if he could date Sam. So, I asked a few questions like; "is this just a courtesy question?" and "are you going to date her even if I say no?" He responded, "if you say no, it's no." Then I asked "what if she says no?" Ron's response was "that would really suck after talking to you." Of course, I said yes and now they are a happy family.

Darby didn't want to go to college; instead, she joined the Army. I believe that many young people join the military and then after the first week, start questioning their decision. They soon realize that it is not as fun as TV commercials depict it to be. She broke her arm halfway through Basic Training and called me up in a state of distress. I told her not to jump the fence, this will pass. I think that may be a difficult concept to comprehend when you're young. There's a saying I believe from King Solomon that has frequently comforted me in stressful situations and also helps me appreciate what I have. It rings true and can be applied in good and bad times, *"This too shall pass."* I was able to obtain her Sergeant's phone number and persuaded him that the best place for her to recover was at home and that I'd return him a great soldier. To her surprise, she found herself on a plane the next day headed home for 30 days. She ended up having to redo Basic Training and finally graduated. I know my dad was very proud and of course I was too. She would marry Matt and have Maddie, my granddaughter and first mate. Matt would end up passing and she ended up moving to Orange County by me. Now Aaron and her do home remodeling and are busy creating businesses, maybe someday I'll see them on Shark Tank.

Big Changes in 17 so Don't Blink

It was Saturday, January 21st, 2017. Steve and I strolled down to Tortilla Republic for a margarita. Rafael made one of the best margaritas in Laguna Beach. Minutes later two girls with the same idea, Kerry and Jenny came in and sat down beside us. Being a social person, I introduced myself to Kerry, while Steve chatted with Jenny. As the evening progressed, we went next door to Skyloft for some music and dancing. At that point, I was much more drawn to Jenny than Kerry. Jenny was a great dancer, seemed down to earth and we clicked. At one point the girls headed to the restroom, I turned to Steve and said, "Jenny really does it for me, do you mind if I ask her out?" He didn't mind, so I just needed to find the right moment to ask for her phone number. Before we left, she took my phone and entered her number into it. I called her shortly thereafter and asked her out, but it still took a couple of weeks to get her to meet me for dinner. We went to Bandera's on our first date in CDM, now comes the part where I say the rest is history. I assume we hit it off since now she's my wife.

For being such a great wingman that night, I felt Steve deserved recognition. So, I had a brass plaque made, similar to one placed on benches at Heisler Park in memory of someone that has passed. Heisler is one of my favorite places in the world. It's in Laguna Beach next to the ocean. You can take a leisurely walk, listen to the waves crashing and have meaningful conversations. It's a Zen place. The plaque read: *Wingman of the Year, Steve, for unselfish service in the line of fire, 2017.* Jenny and I slipped over to the park one late night and mounted it on a bench. The next morning Jenny, Steve and I went for our morning Hiesler walk. I sat down to tie my shoe and wow what is this…a plaque with Steve's name on it. He was surprised! The plaque remained there for over a year until the city painted the bench and evidently some city employee discovered that it was unauthorized. I did give him a trophy after it was pulled off that he still has. So, 2017 started off as a good year.

On our first Valentine's Day, I took Jenny to Heisler Park with a bucket of Kentucky fried chicken, a bottle of Rombauer wine, a blanket and a good playlist then we watched the sunset. Life is not about fancy things or money; it's about experiences. That brought a smile to her face and we had a great time, so that became a tradition for years to come. Later, we would attend the New Orleans Jazz Festival, visit Nashville, see Sheryl Crow in Washington, take motorcycle rides along the coast, James Taylor in Vegas, enjoy the Monterey Jazz Festival, Jack Johnson at the Hollywood Bowl, wine tasting in Paso Robles, boating to Catalina, along with many other fun experiences.

My daughter, Darby, lived in Washington when her husband Matt passed away, also at that time she was in the process of getting out of the Army. About a year earlier they had my granddaughter, Maddie. I suggested that she to move to Laguna Beach, Darby's initial response was, "it's expensive." My reasoning, which I thought made sense was, "So is daycare for a one-year-old. I'll provide free daycare while you go to college." Also, they would be closer to family. I was still operating PWT and would drive to our offices a couple of times a week. We now had three office's in Redlands, Placentia and another in Glendale. If you know anything about Southern California traffic, getting to those locations at times was brutal. Therefore, I tried to work remotely a few days a week and that flexibility also helped me with Maddie. Maddie and I would go to the beach, paint, plant flowers, listen to music and read...one of her favorites was *"Go Dog Go."* She's now in fourth grade and reads at a High School level, so I guess sparking that interest in reading was a good thing.

There was a company, Waterlogic, that I had met with several times over the years to discuss selling PWT. One day, Josh from Waterlogic contacted me and asked me to name my price. I did, but not unexpectedly he said it was too high. Well, that's how many negotiations start. In my mind our price wasn't too high; they just needed more information. I had considered selling for a few reasons. I was fifty-seven, healthy and had a lot of things on my bucket list. With the money and free time, I could help my family, buy a house on the coast, reduce the time spent driving in congested traffic, along with eliminating any employee, customer and legal issues that come up from time to time. Finally, I could purchase that high-end coffee maker that I had always wanted.

When you are conducting business in California, there is significant liability if you or one of your employees make a mistake or has an accident. One-time Eddie, my Service Manager called me and shared that

Damon one of our Service Technicians had an accident, I figured fend benders happen, not a big deal. Eddie then he said Damon hit a person, what do you mean hit a person? He shared that it was guy in a crosswalk, my response was…oh can it get any better? Well, yes it can, the guy was in a wheelchair crossing as Damon was turning right on a red light. Yep that's bad. Believe to or not people here are quick to sue for the smallest things, such as running them over in a crosswalk. A few weeks later I remember I was on my way to the Redlands office when Mike called me and informed me that we had just been legally served for $18,002,345. That's $18 Million, with a capital "M." The $2,345 was for the wheelchair, the rest was for medical bills, pain and suffering. Our insurance was State Farm so I sent them the lawsuit and one of their lawyers contacted me immediately. During the call I asked the lawyer if we went to court could we ask for a discount since the guy was already in a wheelchair, the phone went dead silent for a minute. Evidently the lawyer didn't realize I was kidding, I knew it was a bad situation and we just had to do our best to weather it out. We were covered at that time for up to $4,000,000, which I greatly increased after the lawsuit was finalized. We settled a year later for $1,000,000, which State Farm paid. Just one bad accident can wipe you out, which was another good reason to sell.

When entering a negotiation, consider whether you are in a position of power or weakness, if you have ample time or need to act quickly, these are key factors to be aware of order to have a position outcome. I felt like I was in the driver's seat; Waterlogic wanted PWT and it didn't matter to me if it sold this year or in a few years. During my calls with Waterlogic, there were times when I would excuse myself by saying, "I need to get back to my granddaughter; let's continue our discussion tomorrow." I was in no hurry and they needed to know that. After about six months, we agreed on a price that was very close to my original asking amount. On December 30th, 2017 Waterlogic came to my Redlands office, placed their laptop on my desk, booted it up and I pushed the ENTER button transferring all the money for the sale of the company into my bank account. The company was sold and deal was done. I had committed that if we sold, I'd take care of my key employees. They received over two and a half million dollars since they were instrumental in building PWT, then I sailed away into the sunset. Of course, I had to buy a boat to do that, so I did.

Press release:

Waterlogic, a vertically integrated global designer, manufacturer, distributor and service provider of drinking water systems, is pleased to announce the acquisition of Pure Water Technology, Inc. (PWT) a leading provider of workplace bottleless water in the Southern California market. PWT is headquartered in Redlands, California with two additional depots. Waterlogic will maintain these locations as it bolsters its presence in Southern California. The founder and owner, George Squires, started the business in 2006. The company can be found at www.ditchthebottle.com. The acquisition adds over 6,000 machines in the field to Waterlogic's existing USA operations.

"We have long admired George's operations in Southern California. George built an A+ business and was able to build significant scale without sacrificing customer service". – John Pavlovich, COO, Waterlogic Americas

"My relationship with the M&A team at Waterlogic goes back several years. They were patient and open with me as I grew my business. While I never knew if or when I would sell, I always knew that Waterlogic would be one of the best options for me, my team, and our customers if that time came. I am satisfied with the transaction, how smooth the process was, and I'm excited to watch my employees grow their careers through expanded opportunities at an international company". – George Squires, Founder, PWT

Waterlogic's plan was to acquire dealerships and subsequently sell their company. They already had a significant presence in Europe and were expanding in Asia, but I knew they needed to have more of a base in the US. I guess their plan worked.

Wall Street Journal November 08, 2022 $1.425 BILLION FINANCING FOR ACQUISITION OF WATERLOGIC BY CULLIGAN INTERNATIONAL/BDT CAPITAL PARTNERS

Shearman & Sterling advised Morgan Stanley Senior Funding, as Administrative Agent, on a $1.425 billion incremental financing for the combination of Waterlogic Group Holdings and Culligan International. The combined company is majority owned by funds affiliated with BDT Capital Partners, and the firm's co-investors.

2017 was packed with fun, excitement and significant changes.

No More Alarm Clocks

The next year was a period of adjustment. I wasn't working; instead, I was looking after Maddie and educating myself on how to invest the money from the business for retirement. Retirement planning is something they never teach you in school but should. After reading, doing my homework, attending seminars and talking to friends/advisors, I believed that I had a game plan. First, as I mentioned earlier, I bought a fancy coffee maker. It wasn't a significant investment, but it's probably a wise choice compared to daily visits to Starbucks. Then a boat, a bad investment and a money pit, but it was a lot of fun. After evaluating my options, I invested in stocks, a medical building in Indio, made a couple hard money construction loans and an annuity that I believe would sustain me for the next 40 years.

Also, about that time I was trying to potty train Maddie and she was being very stubborn. At one point I thought "maybe she's on to something, should I start wearing a diaper? It would be really convenient; I'd save all that wasted bathroom time." I'm a logical guy so just do the math; if you're in the bathroom 15 minutes a day, that's 91 hours a year, which is about 3.79 days a year, over 50 years that's 189.5 days, kind of makes sense. Think of all the other stuff you could accomplish…still think I'll pass on that idea. One day she was on my boat without diapers and she pee'd on the bow. That was it! I told her that she pee'd on my toy and I was going to pee on all her Barbie's. One thing I always told my managers is that if you say something you need to follow through and do it or you lose all credibility. Whether you are managing employees or kids, I believe in many ways it's the same. Maddie really didn't like hearing that and promised she would never do it again, so I made a one-time exception to my rule and gave her one last chance. Darby called me the next day and asked what I did? From that day forward she never wore a diaper. Communication 101; if you can find out what's important to a person, you have a much greater chance of success in getting their attention. Evidently having clean Barbie's was very important to her.

The next big purchase was a house in Dana Point, California. It was a fixer-upper, but had a prime location and fantastic views. The interior was straight out of the 70's, featuring over 80 linear feet of floor-to-ceiling mirrors on the walls that would make your head spin. It also had termite damage, glass bathroom doors (don't ask me why), and a number of other issues that most people would have run from. In fact, even though it was in a prime location it sat on the market for 60 days without an offer, so I make a cash offer of about a quarter million off asking price and bingo got it. Nothing that a little hard work, some cash and a sledgehammer won't fix, I had a vision. It became my project and my creative palette for the next eight months. From the house we could walk to excellent restaurants and down to the boat in Dana Point Harbor. Taking day trips on it to Catalina, Newport, Oceanside and Laguna Beach or simply relax and watch the sunset. Maddie was my first mate and we would clean the boat together or drive up to Laguna Beach to the park. Enjoying a simple life without any business meetings or major issues.

In 2018, I took a motorcycle ride over the Blue Ridge Mountains, cutting across on the Tail of the Dragon highway. The Tail of the Dragon is 11 miles with 318 curves. Over the years a total of 29 people have died while riding it. Then we traveled up the east coast going through upstate New York with beautiful rolling green hills and sweeping curves. Finally landing in Niagara Falls, an impressive sight, with 3,160 tons of water flowing over it every second. In the past, I think it was around 2001, Jeff and I had ridden through the Rockies. Back then I wished I could have done more activities like that, but I was a busy guy with kids and work. Now

I have the time and money to have fun. It was the beginning of annual rides with Jeff, Mike, Dave, Arsen and later Paul, Enrique, and John...Maddie calls them the "Crew."

The Bucket List and the Big Ask

One day, Jenny and I were sitting at 230 Forrest Restaurant in Laguna Beach when I asked her what was on her bucket list? I wish I had kept that bar napkin that I wrote the list on. Jenny wanted to do a few things such as go skydiving and to visit Italy. On her birthday that year, we jumped out of a plane. Surprise, surprise!

Now that the house was livable, all the kids were self-sufficient and work was in my rear-view mirror it was time to see the world. First stop, Italy. We visited Venice, Florence, the Amalfi Coast and Rome. My plan was not only to help Jenny check that off her bucket list but also propose to her. Rick is a great friend who I met in Palm Desert and just happens to be a jeweler. He took me to the LA Jewelry District and helped me choose a beautiful stone. Then, he crafted a ring based on a design I had drawn up, featuring an beautiful diamond with rubies encircling the band, symbolizing Jenny's birthstone. I had to carry the ring around and keep it safe until I found the perfect place to pop the question.

One night in Florence, on the Ponte Vecchio Bridge under a full moon I thought, "this is the perfect place." There was a guy there who we had seen the night before playing his guitar and singing. I pulled the ring out of my pocket and held it discreetly in front of me to clear the people around him, dragging Jenny reluctantly through the crowd. Then everyone fell silent. The crowd and musician knew what was coming next, but Jenny was still unaware. She had no idea what I was up to, I dropped down on one knee and asked. She was speechless and surprised, then she said YES. After that my dad said I needed to ask her again when we were back in California because I had her at a disadvantage, I was holding the return plane tickets. By the way, she said yes in California also. Out of all the places we visited in Italy, Florence was our favorite. It had great art, history, people, wine and value, and now it holds beautiful memories. I expect that we will be back there someday.

In 2019 for my 60th birthday Jenny put together a surprise party. Jenny is organized and loves parties so this was right up her ally. I was sitting in El Torito restaurant and here walks in Rod, Terry, Jeff and Rich, friends from 40 years plus that came 1,800 miles, what a surprise! Then we had local friends from near and far join us at the house, well over a hundred people that helped me celebrate being 60 years young. What a treat, more than I expect or probably deserve. Guess I need to plan something big her for her 60th, luckily I have a few more years to plan it. Also, as a birthday present Jenny had a painting commissioned by a famous local artist, Robert Schaar of the Ponte Vecchio Bridge, the place I asked Jenny to marry me.

My travels that following year included a motorcycle trip with the "Crew" to New Orleans. While traveling through Texas we encountered hard rain and unnerving thunderstorms, with lighting hitting next to us on both sides on the road. We're like the mail service, rain or shine we keep going, but the fun factor declines when you're soaked. We finally made it to New Orleans, which I think is one of the most interesting and fun cities in the U.S. Followed by riding some beautiful back roads through Arkansas and the Ozarks with Jeff and my brother, Paul. In my opinion, the best way to explore this country is on a motorcycle.

Tom, my old "partner in crime," contacted me in 2019, I believe he found me through LinkedIn and we reconnected. I flew up to Snoqualmie, Washington, were he was living, a beautiful place in the summer, but buckets of rain coming down for about three months straight in the winter. Then Tom and Sallie came to Dana Point and we took a helicopter to Catalina Island flown by Lorenzo Lamas (the actor), which the girls loved and we had a blast. Based on my math I've known Tom for over 50 years. With some of the things we did and the risks we took we're just lucky to still be walking the earth today. Life is good.

Family Picture 2012

Allie and Grandpa Carl in his swing

Family in the backyard of Yucaipa

George with Mike and Daniel in Mexico

Grandma Irene, George & Bob visting

Suba diving the Great Barrier Reef

PWT Christmas party
at the Mission Inn

Meet Pete

PETE'S RESUME

POSITION: Seeking an opportunity with a quality company to help control cost, promote environmental responsibility, increase productivity and improve safety. Will provide pure drinking water with minimal compensation.

EMPLOYMENT HISTORY: UPS, Toshiba, Lowe's, The Irvine Company, Converse, State Farm and the Better Business Bureau (1,000's of additional references available upon request).

EDUCATION: PhD in Water Purification Technology, with special studies in Cost Containment and Safety.

SKILLS: Team player that works well with ice and coffee systems. Daily self cleaning and complete system monitoring with 2010 state-of-the-art technology. I come with my own health plan and never need a vacation. Enjoy working with people and can improve employee health and morale.

Try Pete for FREE and if you like him he'll work for pennies an hour.

DitchTheBottle.com
1-888-790-7873
Pure Water Technology

Meet Pete Marketing Campaign

Darby graduating Basic Training

Samantha graduating Cal Baptist for Nursing

Kim, Victoria and George in Cabo

Standing in North Korea...for 30 seconds

With the boys in South Korea

Thailand with my new pet

Killing Fields
Unbelievable
atrocities

George and Mark riding in Cambodia

Carl at home with his Tractor

George, Carl and Paul

Allie and Meiko
(one fearless, smart, big cat)

Ride to the Golden Gate during
Covid, the place was a ghost town

Catalina Pet Cemetary

Thanksgiving in St Louis 2016

Ride to New Orleans, then up through the Ozarks

January 21, 2017 at
Tortilla Republic,
I just met Jenny a
few minutes ago

Steve's Wingman Plaque

Guilty of unauthorized plaque mounting

Skydiving on Jenny's Birthday...check that off the Bucket List

Cutting the curves and with the "Crew" on Tail of the Dragon

Dave, Mike, Arsen
George and Paul
on a ride in Arkansas

Jenny and George at the beach

Planting flowers with
Maddie in Laguna Beach

Dana Point house before

Creating an
"open floor plan"

Dana Point house after a little TLC and blood

Maddie and Papa George

Having fun with Maddie

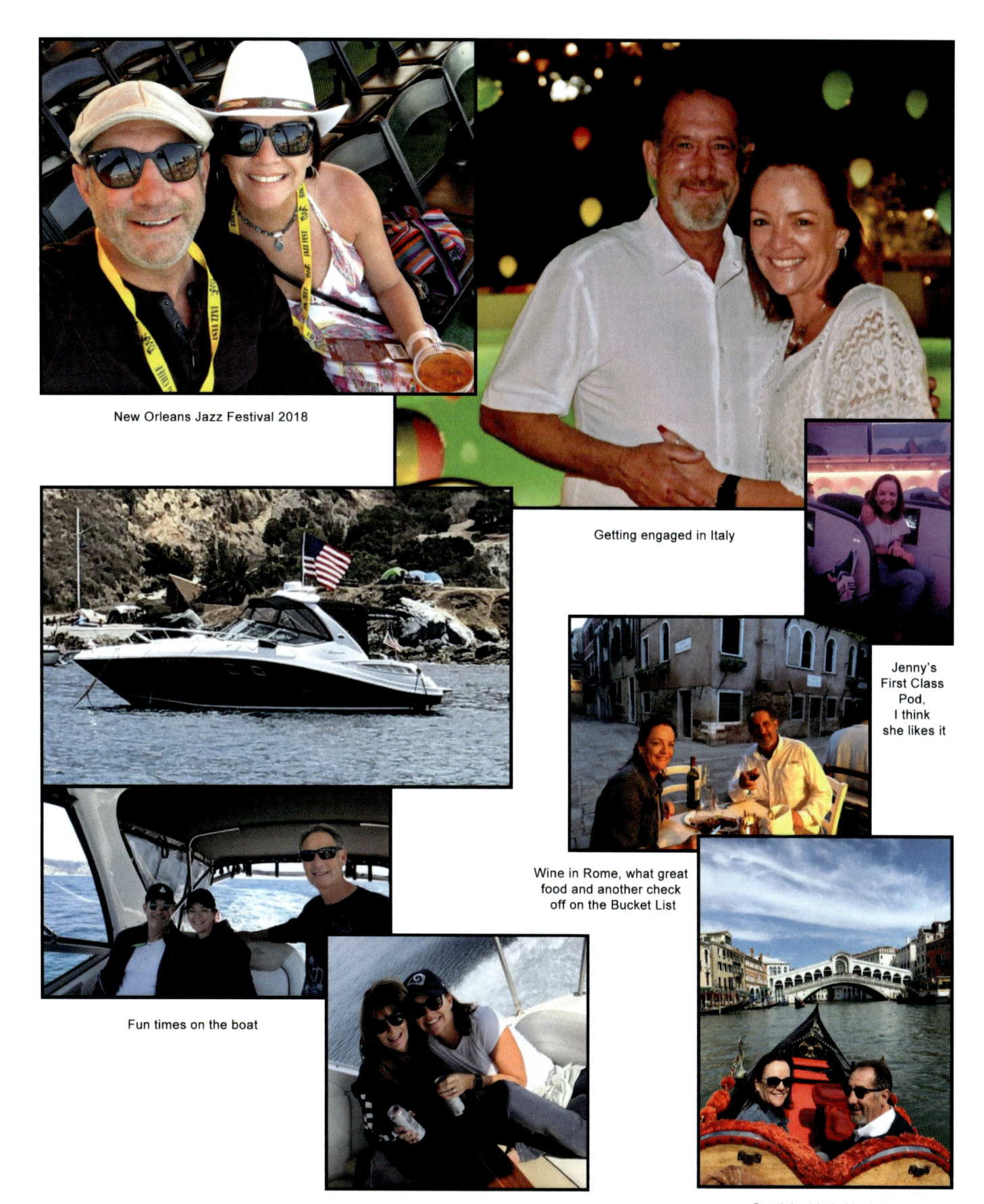

New Orleans Jazz Festival 2018

Getting engaged in Italy

Jenny's First Class Pod, I think she likes it

Wine in Rome, what great food and another check off on the Bucket List

Fun times on the boat

Gondola ride in Venice

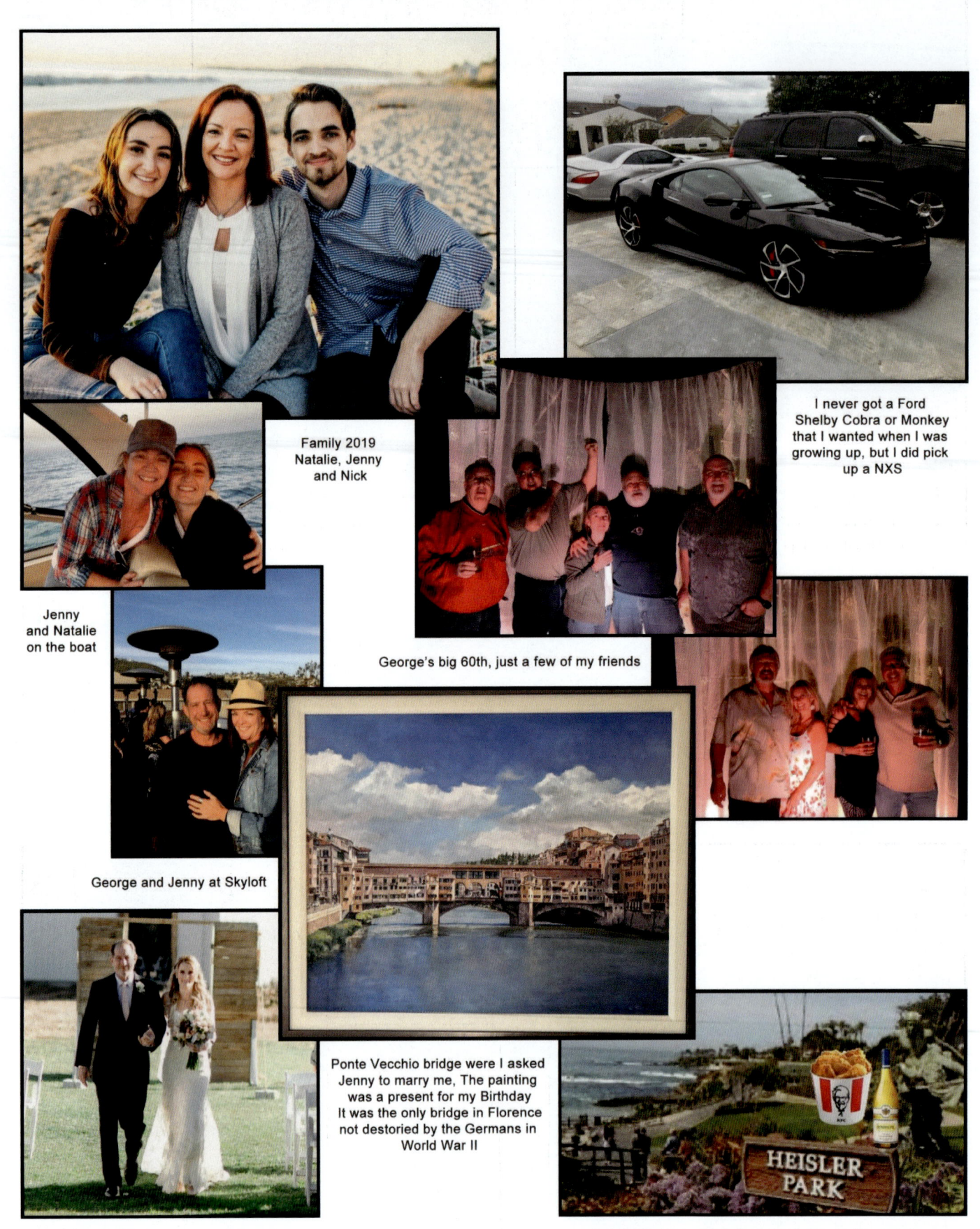

Family 2019
Natalie, Jenny
and Nick

I never got a Ford
Shelby Cobra or Monkey
that I wanted when I was
growing up, but I did pick
up a NXS

Jenny
and Natalie
on the boat

George's big 60th, just a few of my friends

George and Jenny at Skyloft

Ponte Vecchio bridge were I asked
Jenny to marry me, The painting
was a present for my Birthday
It was the only bridge in Florence
not destoried by the Germans in
World War II

Giving Samantha away, sorry Ron "as is" no refunds

Heisler Park one of my favorite places on the planet

Chapter 7

The 2020's - Covid, Mom, Dad, Wedding and Adventures

WHEN COVID HIT, INTIALLY EVERYONE WONDERED how bad would it really be? The banks stopped lending, similar to 2009. It wouldn't have been a big concern, but I had a hard money loan with a group of investors on a $12,000,000 house in Laguna Beach that was in escrow. Since there was no title yet to secure the way I structured my collateral was to have control of the entire escrow in case something went wrong, which it did. The banks shut us off and we couldn't perform as the contract stated. The seller wanted to take all the escrow money, which I felt was ill-gotten gains given the situation.

First course of action, as with all legal matters that I've been involved in is to try to reason with the other party, but I had no success. Their lawyer shut me down right away. In most major agreements, there is a clause called Force Majeure. It's included in contracts to absolve liability for unforeseeable and unavoidable catastrophes that disrupt the expected course of events and hinder participants from fulfilling obligations. This clause covers natural disasters, acts of God and catastrophes. Such as war, earthquakes and pandemics...bingo. My lawyer, Tom, said that very few people have used Force Majeure since World War II or 1918 flu pandemic, but I thought it fit the situation. Here's where you need to feel confident that you have a good case because you're investing more money that you may never see again. There is always a chance of losing and collecting zip. The other party threated me, they said it would cost me money and time if I choose to litigate against them, well, I had both. The other investors didn't want to risk any more money and decided to walk away, but I felt we had a good case. I pursued the lawsuit by myself and ended up collecting more than twice the amount I had invested. They should have been fair and refunded my money, it was a reasonable request. In any lawsuit, no matter how confident feel about your case, *the legal system is not always fair, there is always the possibility of losing. You need to accept that risk.* The hard money lending business is full of rewards and risks. In hindsight, something I wouldn't recommend.

Covid is Here, but Life Doesn't Stop

Jenny moved in with me after returned from Italy. I suppose a true compatibility test is being quarantined together. Just watch Jack Nicholson in *The Shining* and you'll know what I mean. For the first few months we followed the public protocols and even received the vaccinations so I could see my mom and dad.

On July 4th, 2020, I received a call from my brother informing me that our mom had suffered a stroke and that my stepfather, Bob was not in good shape either. He had Alzheimer's, needed a higher level of care and couldn't be left alone. I jumped on a plane the next morning headed for St. Louis. When I arrived, my mom was in the hospital and couldn't speak; she had aphasia. To this day, she is still working hard to recover as much of her language skills as possible.

First, we had to find Bob a another, more secure place to live, so Paul and I started searching. It was during the peak of the Covid pandemic so many places restricted access to their facilities. Dropping Bob off at a doorstep like a puppy in a box just didn't seem right. We found a care facility named Cedarhurst that worked with us and allowed us to enter if we agreed to wear full hazmat suits. Moving furniture on a sticky Missouri day in July when it's 95 degrees and around 90% humidity, while wearing a full contamination suit isn't as enjoyable as it may sound. I believe I shed a few pounds that day. Bob settled in and mom moved in with Paul for the next year. Paul stepped up and has been very involved with mom and Bob. He has done and is doing an outstanding job. Paul's girlfriend, Kathleen, who is great also helps and I believe even more importantly makes him happy.

Mom would eventually move to an independent living facility and Bob continues to regress. He's 95 now and the only person he recognizes just a little anymore is our mom. What a terrible disease. Bob was a Grandmaster at Chess and the Chief Financial Officer of McDonnell Douglas during the race to land a man on the moon. Now he doesn't even know what day it is.

So, are we all getting tired of quarantining yet? Missing all the great local restaurants and live music? We had the boat, which provided a nice escape and Dana Point was less restrictive than most other places. One solution we came up with was hosting small gatherings at the house featuring live music performed by some great local bands looking for a little money and opportunities to showcase their talent. It was a good way to have close friends and neighbors over, help musicians pay their rent, and enjoy good food and drinks. Local musicians, along with great bands such as Missiles of October and Robert Jon and the Wreck, were playing in our backyard. What a treat.

Recovering, Wedding Planning and Travel

Covid was finally winding down or at least stabilizing. That summer, we took our annual motorcycle ride to Seattle, Coeur d'Alene, Bozeman and down to Yosemite; another destination that was on my bucket list. The next year in 2022, we rode to Banff, Canada. The Canadian Rockies are one of the most beautiful places in the world. Everything is clean and pristine, with huge granite mountains raising 12,972 feet touching the sky and the Takakkaw Waterfall that drops a breathtaking 846 feet. Then we rode over to Vancouver and down the coast making a stop in Portland, which was a disaster due to the Black Lives Matter/George Floyd riots along with the large homeless population. Following the riots, over half of the police force resigned. Now they have 554 police officers for a city of 641,000 plus another half million in the suburbs. It's never a good sign when the downtown police station has broken windows and is tagged on every side. Our Uber driver that took us to the restaurant that night warned us that if we were shot or robbed, we should expect a three-hour response time from the police.

Jenny was working as a Nurse Manager at Mission Hospital. Healthcare workers in general were exhausted after dealing with Covid and all the changes taking place in the health care system. It was a stressful position and they wanted her to complete her master's degree at the same time. So, I came up with an idea; quit your job and let's travel the world, then get married in Spain. I had already had plans to go on a motorcycle ride through Spain and Portugal. Jenny was planning a trip with the girls down the Rhine river and we wanted to attend Allie and Dan's wedding in Australia, so why not explore the world.

We sold the boat, which helped fund the adventure and also eliminate a significant expense. If someone ever tells you that boats are fun, believe them. If they say boats are cheap, they're just bold-faced liars. If you have any questions about a Sea Ray boat with twin inboards, feel free to contact me. By the way, when you buy a boat you don't need a license or training in California. They just make sure the check clears and hand you the keys…if they're nice they will wish you luck. So, I had to learn from scratch. Many of the lessons I learned were very expensive, others were simply essential for survival. Case in point; one sunny, beautiful day, Mike, Ruth, Jenny and I were on our way to Catalina Island when the engines died and the emergency alarms came on. I had everyone move up to the front of the boat and when I opened the engine hatch, I immediately saw water flooding the boat; it was already about two feet deep. At that point I had a couple opinions; first somehow find out where the water was coming in from and stop it or second; as Captain Smith of the Titanic said minutes before the ship went down, tell your passengers "do the best for the women and children and look out for yourself." It's challenging to incorporate the word "lucky" in this story, but luckily, I had a pipe on board that enabled me to access and close the incoming port side water valve. The boat was minutes away from sinking. Then I found the broken $1.57 hose clamp that had created this situation and replaced it. I'm a good swimmer, but doing the backstroke for nineteen miles in choppy water would have been pushing it. I pumped the water out and we had a nice lunch in Catalina. Boats are fun, expensive and can be dangerous, especially in the open ocean.

Jenny started working on wedding plans and found Nikki, a fantastic wedding coordinator in Spain. I started working on the travel logistics and on January 2nd, 2023, we set off.

Big World Here We Come

The first stop was North Carolina to see my dad, Carol, then Jenny's dad and his wife, Susan. After that, the globetrotting began. We landed in San Jose, Costa Rica and then drove to La Fortuna, known for its jungles, volcanoes, swinging bridges, zip lines and hot springs. After a week, we headed to the West Coast and discovered a Bed and Breakfast that exemplified the relaxed vibe of Costa Rica called Sueno Del Mar located outside of Tamarindo. A few things you need to know about Costa Rica; the people are incredibly nice, their motto is "Pura Vida," which means Pure Life. Definitely the friendliest people we encountered on our travels. Arnoldo was our ATV guide in Santa Teresa, he's a great guy who we also ended up visiting later and meeting his son. He was very proud that Costa Rica was a "Blue Zone." If you don't know what that is, I'll explain later. He's still a friend with us on Facebook. Maybe someday we can be his tour guide in Southern California. The coffee there is outstanding and the fresh pineapple melts in your mouth, but the roads are terrible. If you rent a car make sure you choose one with high clearance, otherwise you'll end up losing a few parts when you encounter that moon-crater size pothole on the highway.

Next, we made a brief stop in Malaga, Spain to prepare for our wedding. Then we traveled to Australia for Allie and Dan's wedding. In Australia we explored the Gold Coast, the Sunshine Coast and spent a lot of time in downtown Brisbane. On the Sunshine Coast there's a place called Noosa that we really enjoyed, very chill, it feels and looks like you would imagine heaven would, despite it being the home of a landmark called "Hell's Gate." Also, one important thing to know about Australia is that it's very hard to drive there because they use the opposite side of the road compared to here in the United States. We rented a car for a short time, which turned out to be challenging. If you can imagine trying to drive with, someone hitting you with a stick, cars honking, Jenny freaking out and the GPS yelling at you, very confusing…well that's kind of how it felt to me. Time to return the rental car and rely on the reliable Uber system.

Allie recommended that we visit Tasmania on our way to New Zealand. I've never been there, so why not? It was an unexpected gem, with a museum called the MONA and the "cleanest air in the world," because it comes up from Antarctica. Hobart had fantastic food and a great jazz scene. If you ever go there you need to also visit Port Arthur, it's an interesting old English prison where some very bad stuff happened at in the 1800's.

Now off to New Zealand, which ended up being one of our favorite stops. We went to Christchurch, a place that was struck by several major earthquakes, the last one in 2011 that killed 185 people and they are still in the process of rebuilding. Then we headed south to Queenstown, a stunning place that offered one adventure after another such as jet boating, taking a helicopter to Milford Sound, exploring valleys adorned with numerous waterfalls, *The Lord of the Rings* was filmed there. We enjoyed custom cocktails at bars while sitting by large toasty fireplaces, went on a steamboat ride on Lake Wakatipu and wine tasting in the countryside. I wanted to bungee jump but we ran out of time. You may think I chickened out, but I promise next time I'm there I'll do it. By the way, there are two ways to "jump." One; you put on a harness and jump on your own accord; they will not push you. Two; they strap you into a chair with the bungee cord attached to it, tie a rope to the chair and hang you over a thousand-foot drop, then slowly sever the rope strand by strand with a rusty knife until it breaks. Sounds like something from medieval times doesn't it?

At this point, we were improvising our next stops. We knew that in April we needed to be in Spain for my motorcycle ride and Jenny's boat trip down the Rhine. So, Thailand sounds like fun, let's go. We started in Bangkok and then traveled down to Hua Hinn where we hiked to the Phraya Nakhon Cave. It was huge, beautiful and stunning. Money went a long way there, unlike at our next destination.

Originally coming to Australia from Spain, the plane was in the air for over twenty-five hours. It was too long for any plane to travel non-stop, so we stopped in Kuala Lumpur. Even on first class it was brutal. On the way back to Spain, we wanted to break up the flight, so we decided to visit the Maldives. The Maldives is essentially a collection of small islands; a group of 26 atolls and reefs in the Indian Ocean. It's the lowest country in the world averaging only 4'11" above sea level. Our bungalow was situated above crystal-clear, warm, beautiful water. But there's a price you pay for paradise. Over $1,000 per night for the room, $404 for a ribeye steak, so you might want to consider opting for the $45 hamburgers instead. We did some scuba diving, rented bikes and soaked up the sun.

Bike and Boat Trips, then Getting Hitched

Upon landing in Barcelona, Spain we explored the city for a few days before taking a train to Malaga. Out of all the Spanish cities, Malaga was my favorite. It's clean, modern, rich in history, located on the Alboran Sea and is the birthplace of Picasso. It was also a great value, a faction of the cost compared to things here in Southern California.

The "Crew," Mike, Jeff, Gary and I picked up our rented BMW motorcycles' and prepared for the ride. Jenny headed to Germany to meet Patty and Cheryl for a riverboat trip down the Rhine. Jenny shared with me how beautiful Germany was. We may just have to check it out together someday. Then our plan was to meet back at the Marbella Villa in a couple weeks for the big show, our wedding!

We embarked on the motorcycles to explore Spain and Portugal. No guide accompanied us, but we did have a pre-programmed route with all the hotels booked by IMTBIKE, which turned out to be a good choice. We discovered places that we would have never found on our own and stayed in four-star hotels. First, we rode north from Malaga to Granada and Mazagon, then up the Spanish/Portuguese coast to Lagos. There, I had a lobster that was over two feet long, it was delicious. Next, we went to Cascais, near Lisbon where we stayed in an old Portuguese fort on the beach. Off to Evora and Seville, stopping in dozens of historical towns, castles and churches; some were over a thousand years old. The mountain roads were extremely twisty, technical and a lot of fun. At one point, Jeff's front brake broke off, which could have locked up his front wheel and been deadly on those winding roads with cliffs dropping 3,000 feet on one side. IMTBIKE company replaced the motorcycle and we pushed on. Next, Ronda where there is the famous very, very tall "New Bridge" build in 1793; it's 321 feet high and also served as a jail. A couple hundred years ago if you were found guilty of a major crime, they would throw you off the bridge while the townspeople watched, guess they didn't have TV back then for entertainment. It was a spectacular bridge. Then we rode back to Malaga to conclude one of the best rides of my life.

The wedding was next on the list, scheduled for May 10th, 2023. We rented Villa Lampara, which was built by Glenn Tipton, the lead guitarist of Judas Priest. It was a beautiful, tranquil place just outside of Marbella, approximately 50 miles down the coast from Malaga. Given that this was a destination wedding we understood that the cost, distance and time might influence attendance. We ended up having thirty-eight people, all close friends and family. Just to mention a few, there were Jeff, Valerie, Enrique, Lori, Mike, Ruth, Jeff, Nancy, John, Denise, Mike, Jody, Gary, Kim, Todd, Kate, Arsen, Lynn, Bev, Patty, Cheryl, and all the kids: Allie, Dan, Nick, Samantha, Ron, Natalie, Nick, Janelle, Darby, Aaron, Isla, Calvin (still inside Samantha) and Maddie. I don't think we could have asked for more love. A Mariachi band played the day before, by the way I found out Mariachi's are Mexican not Spanish, so that was harder than we thought to pull off but it worked well. Then we had a Spanish guitar during the ceremony. Jenny looked beautiful. A band performed that evening and for the late-night partiers there was a DJ. The following day we just relaxed by the pool to dry out. Much more than I probably deserve in life.

Home, Back to Normal with Good Friends

After visiting seven countries on four continents, flying 43,439 miles in 4 months and 18 days, we finally made it home. Now, back to the daily grind; enjoying Taco Tuesday with good friends, cruising the coast in the convertible, spending days with Maddie, strolling the harbor along with visiting Swallows Inn,

Laguna Beach and the San Juan Capistrano Mission for live music. As Dorothy says in the *Wizard of Oz*, "there's no place like home."

Keeping busy and projects are important when you're retired. So far, I've completed a major remodel on our home and constructed a backyard entertainment area to host parties for a hundred of our closest friends. I also bought a 1961 Corvette to rebuild, a labor of love that has taken a couple of years. It's Maddie's favorite car. I'm currently looking forward to my next project after this book, which is refinishing my dad's swinging bench. My dad recently passed away; I'll share more about that in the following pages. I flew to North Carolina to help Carol, my stepmother, move. Their house is in the country and requires a lot of maintenance, so it made sense for her to relocate to a smaller place nearby in the city of Mathews. When I was there, I took down the bench on the back porch that my dad sat in for 47 years. It was his favorite place in the world, just relaxing and looking out over his beautiful, green back yard, while listening to birds chirping and feeling the cool breeze. I took the bench to the UPS store; it's quite large. They looked at me as if I was asking them to land a man on the Moon and said there was no way they would ship it unless it was in a box. I once saw a coconut mailed from Hawaii without a box, so why not a bench to California. Down the street was an Ace Hardware, so I drove down and presented my situation to some guys working at there. I believe most guys working in a small hardware store are looking for a challenge, some unique problem that entails duct tape and some spare parts from the back room. I also shared with them how much the bench meant to my dad and now me. They helped me create a custom box and later that day I was at the UPS store swiping my credit card for $516. It's going to feel great swinging on it with all the golden memories while looking out over the Pacific Ocean.

Soon after that, I went to St. Louis to visit my mom and Paul. Sam had Calvin in October and Allie had Georgia that following January. Add two more members to the family. Then the "Crew," Mike, Enrique, John and Dave took one last ride of 2023 in Arizona, hitting the Coronado Trail and the Grand Canyon.

In February a group of us lead by Mike and Jody braved what I call the Mexican road of death (it's super narrow, a lot of potholes and busy). We went down to Guerrero Negro, Mexico to pet the whales. It's about half way down the Baja Coast on the Pacific side, what a bucket list experience! The whales are the size of buses and come up beside your small toga boat, then rub against it, roll over and look at you with their eye, as big as a dinner platter and want to be petted like puppies. It's hard to truly describe, you just need to do it if you ever have the chance.

My Dad

On October 5th, 2023, my dad, Carl Edwin Squires passed away, he was eighty-nine years old. I had talked with him about a week before, he sounded weak and out of breath. As I already mentioned he always had lung problems since his younger days in the Air Force. A few days later I called him again, he sounded much better and said he was feeling okay. He also was experiencing arthritis, which made it difficult for him to walk. During our last call we discussed, his health along with Jenny and the kids. At the end of the call, his voice still lingers in my mind, I can still hear him, he said "I love you, Georgie." Those were the last words he ever said to me.

Three days later, Carol called me and shared that he wasn't doing well, and was admitted to the hospital. The next day, I flew to North Carolina and drove directly to the hospital. He was in bed and didn't look well. Carol had been there for the last twenty-four-plus hours, so I relieved her so she could go home to rest while I stayed the night with him. We held hands that night and talked; well, I talked and I believe he listened. The next morning, the doctor came in to take his vital signs. His heart rate and oxygen levels were erratic. He didn't appear to be in pain, so we decided not to administer any medication at that point. Forty-five minutes later, his oxygen level and heartrate began to drop. Paul was driving in from Missouri and was only about fifteen minutes away. I also called Carol and shared with her that she needed to come back. Ten minutes later, he was gone and at peace. I believe he was ready to go. My dad was a pragmatic man who understood that someday we all must leave this world and I believe he had already made peace with that.

I recall visiting my Aunt Ruth a few years earlier. She was the high school prom queen, beautiful, smart, married to a successful businessman and an educator like my mom. In her late sixties, she was diagnosed with arthritis. I thought that having it would just limit your movement and be a little painful. It turned out to be much worse than I could have ever imagined. In her later years, she couldn't move, it was heart-wrenching to see her. At the end, all she could do was talk. I would send her the latest voice-activated devices to help her interact with the outside world, as well as CBD/THC for the pain. The last time I saw her she was completely bedridden and in pain, a mere shell of a person. I thought I could never live like this and then she said something profound that still echoes with me, "George, it's just so hard to live, but it's just so hard to die." She passed away and is free now.

I know we all have to go, but I don't want it to be long and painful. Thank God my dad never experienced that. I hope I never have to make the choice between a life of severe pain and death.

Life's Safety Nets

My dad and mom always have been my safety nets, no matter what! They enabled me to take risks; every day of my life, I always knew I had someone there to catch me if I fell. They provided me with feedback, advice and ideas for many of my situations regarding kids, relationships, employees and business. They always told me if I worked hard, I could do anything; which I believe is important for kids to hear. Also, Allie, Nick, Sam and Darby used them for advice, proofreaders and sounding boards over the years. My dad always believed that graduations were very important and attended all of them. Remember, he dropped out of high school but eventually earned a college degree. I think he was initially motivated by my mom to go to college. He would say, *"It's not where you start, it's where you end that matters."* When someone that close passes away, a piece of you goes with them.

Remembering the Past but Looking Forward

When I get older losing my hair

Many years from now

Will you still be sending me a Valentine

Birthday greetings bottle of wine

If I'd been out till quarter to three

Would you lock the door

Will you still need me, will you still feed me

When I'm sixty-four

...my current ringtone

In the summer of 2024, we rode motorcycles to Canada. I've already shared with you a few rides with the "Crew." I estimate we've ridden about 38,000 miles in the last seven-years, that's one and a half times around the world. Not bad for a bunch of old guys. This last ride is fresh in my mind, so I'll share it and if you use a little imagination, I'd like to take you along.

Check your gas; John, Mike, you and me are hopping on the highway in Orange County California, it's a beautiful day. Then we head north running highway 101 pass San Francisco, I know it's getting hot as we go inland, 536 miles and not much to see…yes, your butt is sore, mine is too, don't complain. The next day let's jump out to the beautiful California coast where we finally have cool weather, I agree that feels so much better! Look at the great sights, ocean views, waves hitting the rocks on the coast, then we come to the huge redwoods and twisty roads. As you hit that 30mph curve doing 60mph, on top of your 800-pound machine and lean in to make the corner I saw your foot peg scrap on the hot pavement...that was a shot of adrenaline for sure. I'm behind you when you reach the middle of the curve, racers call it the apex; you twist your throttle and accelerate forward like a cork out of a champagne bottle. You do that 50 or 60 more times, keeping the shiny side up, oh yeah what fun you're having now!

After that we cut inland to Salem, Oregon for the night, about halfway there you're feeling the heat wave, can you believe it's 118 degrees! I just heard on the news that two motorcycle riders died in Death Valley today from the heat, I agree with you that wouldn't choose to ride there in the July. Hard to think our climate isn't changing. The next stop Tapps Lake to meet up with Gary and Dean. Gary has a house on the lake, jump in the water it feels great. Ok that was a good night's sleep, let's head to Highway 20 in Washington, though the Northern Cascades. Look at the mountains we're heading into, it's sure going to be a beautiful ride with twisty roads, lakes, riding over dams and more great views. Remember me sharing that roads are so aggressive and gets so much snow they close them for eight months out of the year, but you picked the right time because the weather is perfect to cut though Rainy Pass at 5,400 feet. Next stop is Sandpoint, Idaho were Jeff and Doug join us.

Now top off your gas tank and let's start heading up to Calgary Canada. As we cross the US/Canadian border everyone is riding in formation, on the right and left, staggered about 20 feet apart. Nothing you haven't done hundreds of times before. Yep I see it, on both sides of the road are there are bright yellow Canola flowers, in some places as far as you can see, miles and miles. In Calgary the spouses flew in and are waiting. First let's rest our butts and have a great steak dinner then tomorrow we bought tickets to the Stampede Rodeo, sounds like a blast. It's the largest rodeo in North America and maybe the world. By the way riding a bull bareback shouldn't be on your list of things to do, did you see that cowboy get thrown hard against the rails by a charging bull, that was painful to watch. I think I saw tears in his eyes. In the eight seconds riding, they're bent more ways than a county fair pretzel. Great fun to watch but not to do...of course if you don't want to take my advice let me take out a life insurance policy on you first. As we planned the next day, we'll take a shuttle to Lake Louise and lunch in Banff. Now it's Monday, time for the spouses to jump back on a plane and head home. According to our game plan we point the motorcycles south to Glacier Park.

Go ahead and take the lead. I'm all in for riding the Going-to-the-Sun-Road through the middle of the park, it's a must do. Wow, just cruising between the mountain ranges that were formed 7,000 years ago carved by ice glaciers, with stunning angles that the sun bounces off of is just indescribable. Then we passed by waterfalls, such as the Weeping Wall fed from the melting snow in the middle of summer. It's just a couple feet from the road and over a hundred feet long. Great to ride next to it and feeling the mist on a hot day, you got to enjoy that!

Remember to watch out for deer, we just saw so a few of them next to the road and the girl at the hotel in Salmon, Idaho shared with us that there was just a bad motorcycle accident when a biker hit one yesterday.

Not much to see when we are dropping down into Salt Lake City, let's continue south to Park City for the night and a good meal. Then prepare for the toasty desert going to Las Vegas, 422 miles on a long, a straight boring road, you know it's going to be another sore butt day. One thing about getting back to Southern California there's no cool way to get home. Halfway there at St. George, Utah you need to pull over and let's put on our water soaked cooling vest which helps break the heat and make it to Las Vegas. Gary, Dean, Jeff and Doug had broken off after Glacier Park, but Arsen is waiting for us in Las Vegas.

I agree never let a skinny guy pick out a restaurant, when Arsen goes to an all you can eat buffet they lose money. He always picks out the best steak place in town, so he made us reservations at The Golden Steer. It comes highly recommended and has been in business since 1958; Marilyn Monroe, Frank Sinatra and the Mafioso hung out there, in fact it's in the movie Casino. I'm full after that big steak dinner but if you want to grab a margarita at the Luxor, I'm in. Also, let's hit the show "Postcard from Earth" tomorrow in the new 2.3-billion-dollar Sphere. WOW, wasn't that a great story, effects and overall venue, I agree it was just fantastic!!!!

How early do you want the kickstands up? The earlier the better, so we can avoid some of the desert heat. Wake up, I figure we can grab breakfast down the road, let's get going. Now you turn up *Hotel California* by the Eagles on your bike's stereo, put on an abundance of sun screen, flip down the highway foot pegs and let's ride. After 16 days and 4,234 miles you're finally home safe. I'll just add this, I think you would agree that the people we met in small and big towns along the way were interesting and fun. It was a great ride, thanks. In 2025, we plan to ride the Alps and Southern France. It's a great life!

Today

Allie, Nick, Sam and Darby are all doing well. They are my biggest accomplishments in life and a great source of pride. I now have Jenny and two more wonderful kids with Nick and Natalie, along with Todd, Kate, Ross and Excelda as part of my family. I couldn't ask for a better family and friends. All of them are positive beacons in my life and I believe they'll always be there for me through thick and thin.

My journey is not over yet. If you're counting, I still have 1 of my 9 life's left, maybe I can get a bonus life too… I think that nun I hit me on my motorcycle owes me one. I hopefully have many more years and adventures to come. Sometimes, bad decisions make good stories, but my aspiration is to live compelling narratives through wise choices, surrounded by the people I cherish. Jenny and I aren't done traveling the world; I still have many more motorcycle rides with the "Crew" and Taco Tuesdays with my dear friends ahead. Most of all, I want to witness my grandchildren growing up.

There are areas defined by National Geographic as "Blue Zones" in the world, where people reach the age of 100 at a rate ten times higher than the rest of the world. Remember I mentioned Blue Zones earlier in my story with Arnoldo in Costa Rica. Anthropologists, demographers and researchers have attempted to identify the lifestyle characteristics that could account for longevity. Diet, social network, physical activity, family and a positive attitude were concluded to be key factors.

Sardinia, Italy – home to the world's longest-lived men

Okinawa, Japan – home to the world's longest-lived women

Loma Linda, CA –outlives the average American by a decade

Ikaria, Greece –significantly reduced rates of chronic illnesses

Nicoya, Costa Rica –twice as likely as Americans to reach 90

Maybe my little house in Dana Point on Blue Lantern Street could become the next Blue Zone. We are all here for a finite amount of time, I just want to make the most of it. In the end you can't take any material things with you, but I hope I can take some of my memories. Remember, tomorrow is never promised.

Just so you know; in my will/trust I have $50,000 set aside for a celebration of life party, if you're reading this book you're invited. But of course, you need to outlive me.

I'm writing this for my kids, grandkids, great-grandkids…maybe a few other people will get a kick out of this also.

To be continued…

2022 motorcycle ride,
David couldn't make it so we bought his head on a stick

Bnaff Canada, just a beautiful place

David, Mike, George, Brett and Arsen in Tombstone

Old 2013 Goldwing that has seen many states

Last ride of 2023 Cornado Trial
(when it says 10 mph corner...
it's really 10 mph)
and Grand Canyon with the "Crew"

New Goldwing that will see many states and was on the 2024 Canada ride

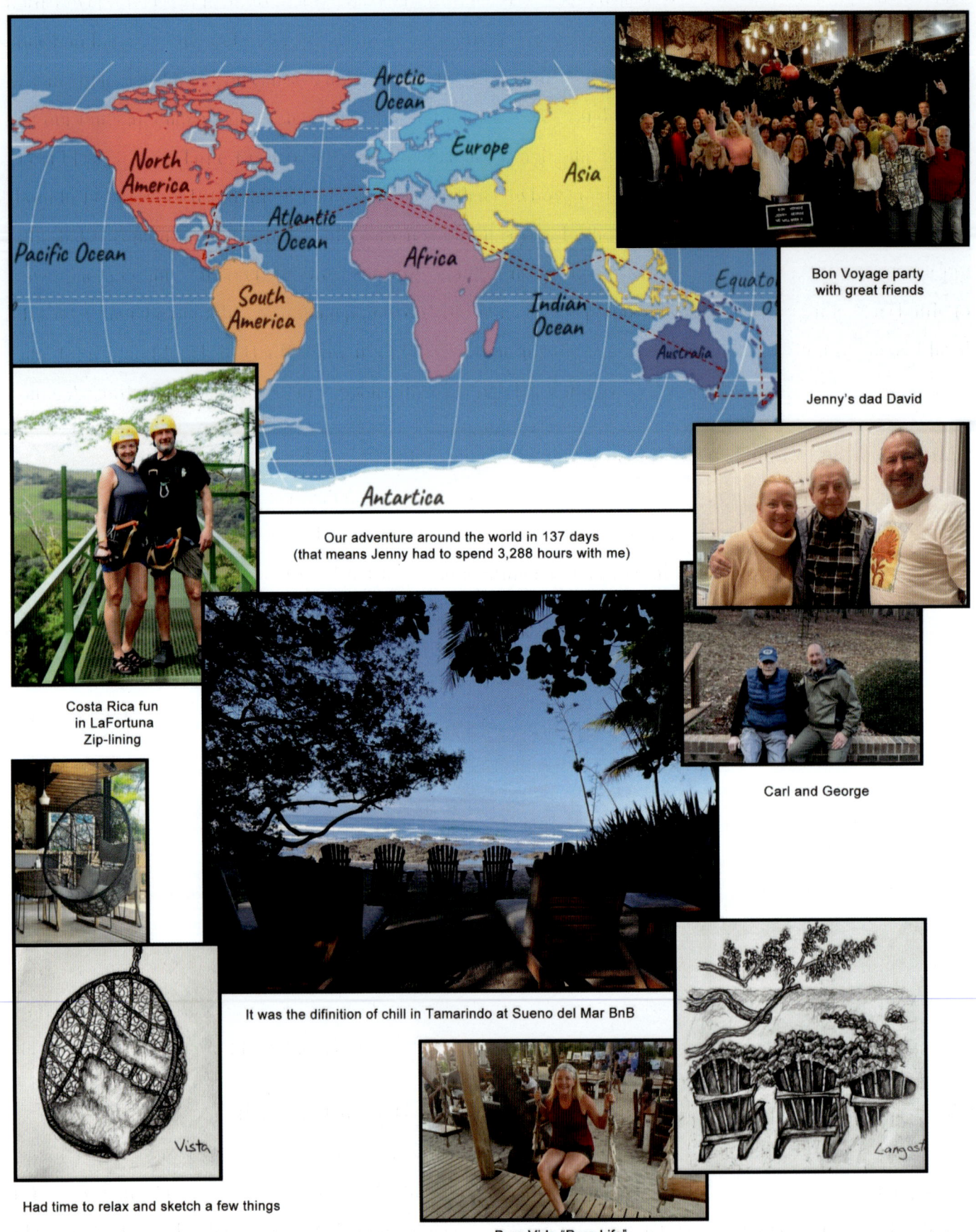

North America

Arctic Ocean

Europe

Asia

Pacific Ocean

Atlantic Ocean

Africa

Indian Ocean

South America

Equator 0°

Australia

Antartica

Our adventure around the world in 137 days
(that means Jenny had to spend 3,288 hours with me)

Bon Voyage party
with great friends

Jenny's dad David

Carl and George

Costa Rica fun
in LaFortuna
Zip-lining

It was the difinition of chill in Tamarindo at Sueno del Mar BnB

Vista

Had time to relax and sketch a few things

Langast

Pura Vida "Pure Life"

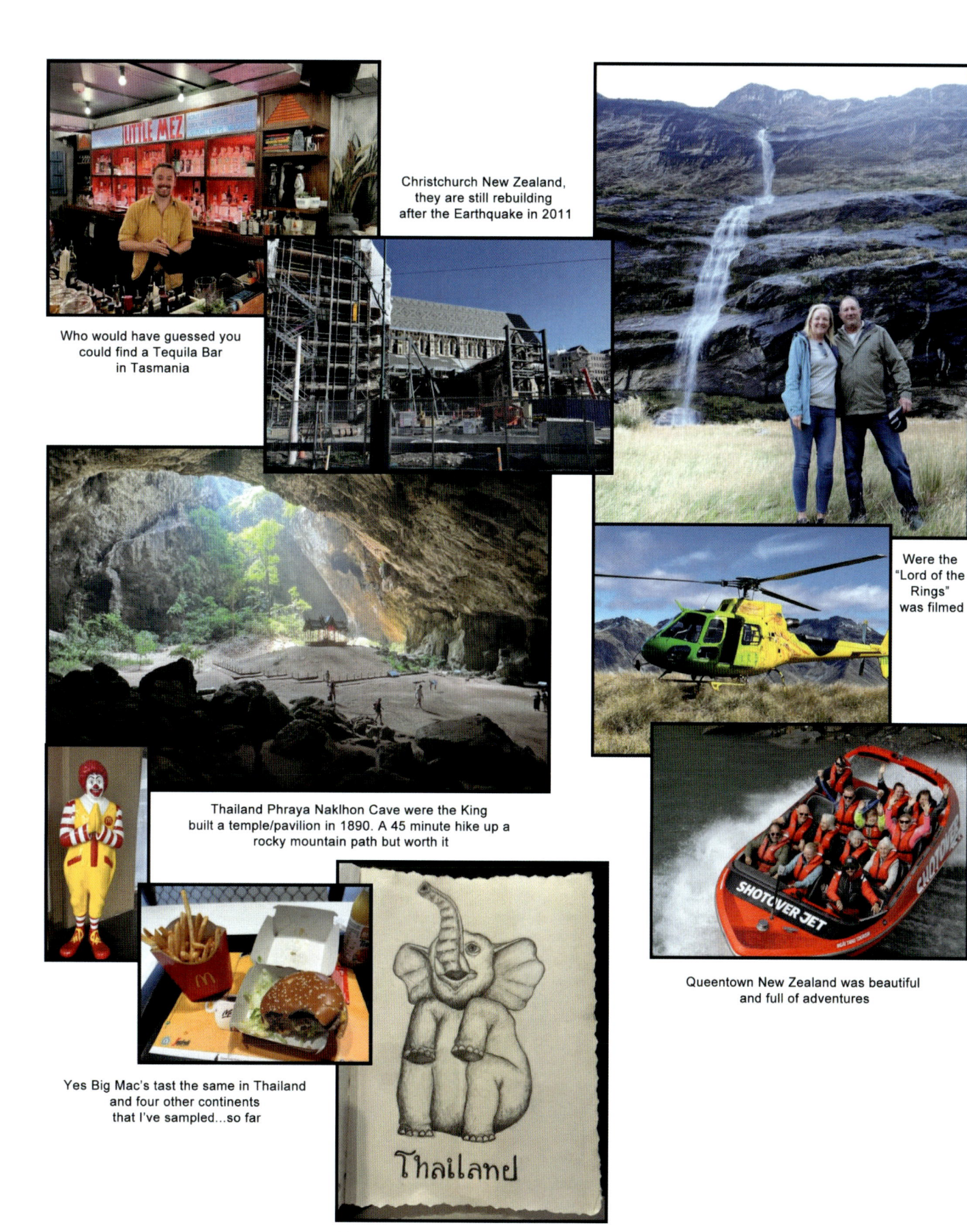

Who would have guessed you could find a Tequila Bar in Tasmania

Christchurch New Zealand, they are still rebuilding after the Earthquake in 2011

Were the "Lord of the Rings" was filmed

Thailand Phraya Naklhon Cave were the King built a temple/pavilion in 1890. A 45 minute hike up a rocky mountain path but worth it

Queentown New Zealand was beautiful and full of adventures

Yes Big Mac's tast the same in Thailand and four other continents that I've sampled...so far

My Sketch of a stone elephant in Hua Hinn

Rocking at the Hard Rock Mildives

Our room in the Maldives over water

Jenny looks happy

Sunset at our island...
does it get any better?

George, Jenny, Valerie & Jeff taking a walk in Malaga,
it's a great city, I could definitly live there

" When visiting an exhibition of children's drawings, some
years later, he remarked: 'When I was their age I could
draw like Raphael, but it took me a lifetime to learn to draw
like them' "

[Roland Penrose, Picasso: His Life and Work, 1958]

Picasso was born in Malaga and a lot of his art is still there

Cathedral of Malaga started 1528 and never finished

Cheryl, Jenny and Patty on thier river boat trip

Riding the Spanish coast

Spain, friendly people, good food and they drive on the correct side

The very tall "New Bridge" in Ronda, the middle was the jail

Rojo River which you probably guessed means Red or Blood

This was one of our Hotels coverted from an old Portugal Fort, how cool

In a Bull Fighting ring

George's dinner

161

The Wedding, what more could we ask for!

The day before having fun

Just hitched

Just some of our "Crew" helping us celebrate

George Maddie, Jenny and Isla

Mr and Mrs Squires with Kate and Todd

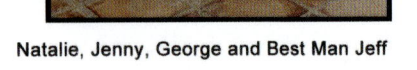

The stunning Wedding Villa

Natalie, Jenny, George and Best Man Jeff

396 Chevy with fuel injection not stock by any stretch

George's project for the last two years, fun projects are important

Concert at the San Jaun Mission

Petting the Whales in Guerrero Negro Bucket List stuff

Marc, Enrique, George and Todd fishing

2023 Santa Claus Ride for charity

Carl Edwin Squires
April 13, 1934 - October 5, 2023

Midland — Carl passed peacefully. He was born to George and Veloney of Efland, North Carolina.

At 18 he entered the US Air Force and served as an electrical technician in North Africa. After his term in the Air Force, he completed his GED, then earned a BA and MA at Arizona State University. Later he earned a Doctorate of Education from the University of Missouri. He said, "it's not where you start, it's where hard work takes you." Carl retired from Central Piedmont Community College after 16 years as a VP/Dean. He also served as a consultant to several colleges locally and internationally.

Carl was a member of the Rotary Club and Lions Club. As a member of Bethel Church Midland, he was instrumental in raising funds for the Sanctuary building.

He built his dream home in Midland and enjoyed home projects. One of his favorite pastimes was sitting on his porch swing enjoying the view and peacefulness.

Carl and his wife Carol of 54 wonderful years enjoyed domestic and international travel.

With a life-long interest in aviation, he flew for many years and was one of the original members of the Desert Sky Riders Flying Club.

Carl leaves behind his wife Carol, along with sons George (a successful businessman) and Paul (a very successful computer engineer). He was very proud of both of them. He also leaves behind his grandchildren: Allison, Nicholas, Samantha, and Darby. He has 3 1/2 wonderful great grandchildren: Maddison, Isla, Calvin with one more on the way. Survivors also include nephews Dan and Douglas and nieces Doris, Carol, Dorothy, Jane, Peggy, and Karla. His life was blessed and full of love.

A Memorial Service will be held at 12:30 on Tuesday, October 17th, at Bethel Church, 12700 Idlebrook Road in Midland, N.C.

In lieu of flowers memorial donations may be made to "Feed the Souls Food Pantry" at Bethel Church Midland at www.feedthesouls.org or a charity of your choice.

Hartsell Funeral Home of Midland is serving the family.

Online condolences may be made at www.hartsellfh.com

My Dad's favorite place in the world

Dexter the friendliest dog on earth and now part of our family

Aunt Ruth in her good times

My Mom 2024

New backyard to entertain close friends
another one of my projects...my design and I'm cheap labor

Gary, Mike, George, John & Dean riding the Northern Cascades

Let's get this ride started, Canada 2024

Stampede Rodeo, go Cowboy

Lake Louise...STUNNING

The Crew with our
Honey's
(I guess John
is taking the picture)

$1,000 on red at the roulette table,
I'm currently a winner 14 out of 18 times
(the key is to think positive thoughts)

POSTCARD FROM EARTH

The 2.3 billion dollar Sphere in
Las Vegas, what an
unbelievable venue and show
"Postcard from Earth"
I would highly recommend it!

Dan, Georgia, Allie and Ava

Georgia (Georgie),
Papa George and Allie
2024

Papa and Maddie in Brisbane

Happy
Isla and Calvin

Sam, Ron and George at Laguna Beach

Home Sweet Home in Dana Point

Life Lessons

The reality is that you control very little in life besides yourself; it's about managing what's thrown at you.

Anything you say can and will be used against you.

It doesn't matter what they believe; it's what we know.

Always believe in your kids.

Trust your intuition; there are always reasons why you feel a certain way.

One of the keys to finding yourself and being successful is to be willing to try things, then adjust or change especially early in life.

Chance favors a prepared mind.

The most important thing in life is having a positive attitude.

Take the money out of the decision and if it changes reconsider it.

If you can't put it on the front page of the newspaper don't do it.

I believe you need to invest in yourself and not wait for someone else to invest in you.

You can be lazy; you can be dumb, but don't be both.

One thing in life you'll never regret is saying thank you.

Before you do, say or write something that has significant consequents, wait twenty-four hours.

Do not let the bad things that happen in your life bleed over and poison the good things in your life, you need to compartmentalize.

Holding a grudge is like holding a piece of hot coal in your hands; the only person it hurts is you. Moving forward and being successful is always the best revenge.

You never want to trade your tomorrow for today.

Productivity is not a matter of how much time you spend working, it's how much you get done.

You cannot justify doing something bad no matter what has been done to you, if it's wrong then it's wrong!

Time is the most valuable thing you will ever have in life.

Embrace mistakes and learn from them, if you're not making mistakes then you're probably not doing enough.

If a person doesn't ask for advice, they probably aren't going to listen.

Tomorrow is never promised.

Being right or even justified isn't always the most important thing as long as you don't compromise your integrity or morals.

You should assess risk according to your current situation and avoid making decisions based on the time or money already invested.

This too shall pass.

When entering a negotiation, consider whether you are in a position of power or weakness, if you have ample time or need to act quickly, these are key factors to be aware of order to have a position outcome.

By the way, one thing about retirement is that you need projects.

The legal system is not always fair, there is always the possibility of losing. You need to accept that risk.

It's not where you start, it's where you end that matters.